EVERGLADING,
or TIME ENOUGH

by Gill Holland

ISBN 978-0-9897544-0-8

LOC 2013913367

www.hollandbrownbooks.com

Interior design by Typecast Publishing
Letterpress and exterior design by Hound Dog Press

Printed in the USA

EVERGLADING

or TIME ENOUGH

by Gill Holland

FOREWORD

Welcome, Dear Reader! The pleasures of reading and remembering are many, making new friends and revisiting old ones. The earliest poems in this collection introduce saints from ancient times. In addition to old timers at Davidson like President Martin and Dean Johnston, Shaw Smith and Bill Hight, you will meet Beulah, Kent, Wally, Vernon, and Mrs. Wagner from Washington and Lee in the fifties, Dr. Eliason at UNC-Chapel Hill, Bob at Redlands, and family from four generations.

We also fly to Classical Chinese times. Along with newer descriptions of un-heroic family misadventures in heroic couplets, translations of Classical Chinese masters will suddenly start up. The author's name will be given in parentheses. They come from as far back as the Confucian Book of Odes up to the Sung Dynasty a millennium and a half later. Bits from the poetics of the Middle Kingdom follow below.

Confucius's stand on the integrity of language is surely a universal imperative. "Overdo your deeds but shame your words down. If your words are not close to your heart you can't do a thing." "Words— just far enough is enough" (Holland, Keep an Eye, 7; Enter Text 5.3, p. 139). Even the ancient sign for "correct, right" shows a foot stopping short of crossing a line" (Wieger, 266).

Perhaps this is the moment to recall Coleridge's argument that Chinese was not an alphabet of letters but a symbolic language based on forms found in nature like water and mountain. He speculated that Adam and Eve spoke Chinese in the Garden of Eden! (Enter Text 5.3, pp. 142-143)

The Confucian elevation of LI (worship, ceremony, etiquette) was accompanied by more spiritual notions of Taoism and Buddhism such as the "branch-hanging antelope." Imagine that an antelope is being pursued by hunting dogs. As they get closer it propels itself up and entangles its antlers in the tree branches. The dogs charge in but can find only the scuff marks left in the dust below. Well, the scuff marks are the words of the poem—the poem is up in the tree! (Enter Text 5.3, p. 144)

Finally, the heroic couplet. How do Eastern quatrains merge with Western couplets? For years at Davidson College the three-week July Experience has opened the door to rising high school juniors and seniors to discover the pleasure of writing original heroic couplets within the straits of twenty "characters," that is, syllables arranged in two lines of riming iambic pentameter. (The iamb is two syllables accented weak-strong; pentameter is five such iambs.) Here are couplets by two rising high school seniors that present within this straightened harness skill and delight:

> A Lazy Summer Afternoon
> by Kate
>
> The sun, lounging lazily in the air,
> Yawns as it plays with shadows in my hair.
>
> On My Mind
> by Jack
>
> Slinking 'cross the green'ry, toes bathed in dew,
> My thoughts not yet athinking, yet they think of you.

The trochees (strong-weak, known as the "headlong foot") substituted for the iamb in "Yawns as" and "Slinking" give a "headlong" shove to open the line. In the second line Jack substitutes an alexandrine (six iambs) to great effect. In a draft (the class was all working at the blackboard) we deleted syllables and words to determine whether or not the same effect could be caught in ten syllables and decided the alexandrine should stand. A Chinese saying comes to mind: One must "never draw feet on a snake" (Lai 58). Do not add superfluous words to what is complete. But we let the extra iamb stand.

Let us close with another Chinese saying: "To welcome a guest with shoes put on hurriedly the wrong way (to show great welcome to a guest)" (Lai 121). Welcome to *Everglading*!

ACKNOWLEDGMENTS

Works Cited

Holland, J. Gill. "China and the hieroglyphical Chinese language in the imagination of Coleridge." *Romantic Geographies: Proceedings of the Glasgow Conference*, September 1994. Ed. Colin Smethurst. Glasgow, 1994. Pp. 287-294.

----- *Keep an Eye on South Mountain: Translations of Chinese Poetry*. Davidson, NC: Briarpatch, 1986.

-----"Teaching Narrative in the Five-Character Quatrain of Li Po." *Enter Text 5.3 (2005-2006)*. Web.

Lai, T. C. *Selected Chinese Sayings: Translated and Annotated*. Hongkong: University of Hongkong Book Store, 1960. Print.

Wieger, L. *Chinese Characters*. 2nd ed. (1927) Trans. L. Davrout. New York: Dover, 1965.

Some of the poems in this collection appeared earlier in the following books: *Keep an Eye on South Mountain: Translations of Chinese Poetry* (Briarpatch, 1986), *Pocahontas and the Drunken Waiter* (Briarpatch, 1979), *The Tao Comes to Davidson.* (Briarpatch, 1994). Some appeared in local and regional literary journals and in *The Christian Science Monitor*.

My wife Siri and I dedicate this collection to our children and grandchildren and to the memory of onkel Bjørn. Special thanks are given to the late Dean John M. Bevan for his encouragement and support of our venture into the Chinese language and culture. We must also express our gratitude to the late Moreland Hogan, publisher of the Briarpatch Press, for bringing these earlier collections into the public world. Many thanks go to Stephanie Brothers at Holland Brown Books and Jen Woods at Typecast Publishing for their help in preparing this typescript for publication.

—Gill Holland

TABLE OF CONTENTS

A BOY

THE MOUNTAINS

BURLESQUE BUDAPEST

WAR FEVER

DOLPHIN IN OUR WOODS

HOIST A SAIL

ROLL THE STONE AWAY

A RESTLESS MOURNER

BUFFALO WATCH OUR EYES

THE TAO COMES TO DAVIDSON

TAKING OFF

CASABLANCA, OR: TIME ENOUGH

A BOY

A BOY REMEMBERS TOSCANINI'S LAST VISIT TO RICHMOND

After Respighi the encores, and the last:
Dixie in the Mosque!
Oh, we cheered that encore,
when a god stooped to enter our house door

and eat at our table.
My father said he rolled down the Appian Way that night
through all the fountains right into wet Richmond.
We did weep.

The papers reported he stepped down soon after
wandering from the score.
But when he threw that baton and shouted an oath
it sailed like a seabird

all the way to Rome.
He could see all the way
like sunup over ruins

to march Caesar's legion once again.
Then Dixie in the Mosque!
He used a little table salt
and we fell like rabbits in a box.

At the backstage exit light we waited
to cheer more. A top hat and a white face
if you stood on your tiptoes,
our tired Maestro headed

to the limousine
driving as though he were on wheels
through the heads of the dark crowd.

CHRISTMAS UNCLES

The Christmas uncle arrives once a year.
He won't bring a single white shirt

for Mother's Virginia parties, hasn't come to see those people
but just to put the star at the top of the tree.

At bedtime he trains the children to spell asafoetida
and battalion and dream of fighting marlin

and shooting sharks. Older he'll teach some other tricks
he promises. He never will. Nor explain why one year

he comes in a long Packard and the next on a bus ticket
with different matching ladies each time.

The one with ribbons is nice, but the other has
a fox who sleeps biting his tail

and would nip your nose if you waked him up.
Maybe the Christmas uncle will teach the children his fingers,

how they trick the fox, spell words
with his hands, shuffle

the secret deck of cards kept in the drawer with socks
after his last visit.

TATTERS

Fritz, my second dog, warmer of his master's feet, comes up in
          conversation today.
In the present form of another corporal of dachshund persuasion
so well preserved for eleven—not a hint of gray in his muzzle—
we allow it's Grecian Formula for hue and olive oil baths for gloss.
Discussing the weather he and I agree in balloons
it just isn't November, this spring day, but sure as sin
somewhere in the neighborhood Mr. Winter broods in Svengali's
brows.

Fritz slept years ago as blind under the covers by the boy's feet
as headed to Garland-Rodes Elementary under the final wheels of
the
          Bedford Avenue Express,
their missions having mixed, straight lines and wavering.
His predecessor, Blackie, the first dog, obsidian of eye and heart, I
had held
          by a twisting collar
and beaten with the handled hairbrush on obedience days.
He was a cocker we gave away to the Houcks
the April Daddy, uniformed, stepped out the door to do his stint
          for the Allies.

A SILHOUETTE OF HATS
UNDER BLACKWATER CREEK BRIDGE, LYNCHBURG

A tramp of one hat or one coat and something like trousers
counts cars in the railway keep
to straighten out the multiplication of the universe.

In the beginning was on his fingers. His station is
in mashed grass by the Dixie Limited, the western line.
On an elbow he observes a train that rolls into the yard.

Stop beside him and ask, What is your work?
Roll call car after car after clickety-clack
and never miss a digit of a serial number of a moving box.

I made my mind to catch each
like knocking off hard hats one by one
from a slow gaining freight with a rifle.

He intones them onto the big board of lights,
the whosoever who scrapes match after match
on the sole of great hobo's shoe in the sky.

Who doesn't follow smoke up?
Whatever grisly foreign matter we may burn in the eye of the bridge
the smoke the earth releases rises to the heaven it can find.

If you've lain down and looked up at Jericho's head
(while the others are reciting Sterno)
against the night you'll know these silhouettes,

the dog's head as dark as a shut-down furnace at Reusens.
When Sammy from Richmond fainted and pushed his chum's hand
in the fire with the cans nobody noticed

until we woke up, the wrist that he left
little more than the cabbage burnt on Sunday.
It could have been the doctor called to heal him

who took the same path, or his judge Tuesday,
or the clerk who sold the first man his suit.
This half the world anyway's full of strange candles to burn down.

You catch the melt you can
in any loose palm that's sidled into town.
One good beano and don't need any more hair to burn.

After quick Christmas it's hades and the ribs of this night bridge
glaring over Blackwater Creek.
In these convoys calm comes with keeping the numbers straight.

In spite of what happens in tramp camp
men want better.
Stick a hook in the back of any hobo

and he'll help you catch dinner as quick as a grasshopper.
We're on the banks of the right river James—
who could get a place sweeter if the numbers were right?

I moved on and left him
memorizing figures as if
in the beginning all was number.

REVEILLE JAMBOREE

To spite the bugling in the name of sleep sufficient
while a thousand scouts were upstanding to salute Valley Forge
I stayed deeply slugabed within my bag.
This is not a dictatorship. It's a free country.

Our scoutmaster ex-sergeant ex-marine whatever
whatsoever entered the tent and the picture.
In a jiffy, soon, my hands, rear, elbows, ego
were scrubbing the insides of the garbage can, a filthy thing.

Thomas Carlyle, Victorian heavy, preached
bringing order to the task outside
orders what's inside best.
Forge new valleys Forge, salute Old Glory uprising.

Too sheltered to be ashamed for long
we were again trading patches knives
under blue skies of Pennsylvania.
Western scouts had armadillos.

We saw Ike in the parade through hills,
waved. A Texan showing off
a bullwhip
took forty-two stitches up his arm.

Line up, salute Old Glory rising.
I cleaned the bottom of that can
out of sight big ears, elbows, ego somewhere in there,
one lost breakfast that's stuck longer than
the armadillo cute for a day on its leash.

Do, learn one's duty.
Keep an eye out for the honorable way.
Stay off the roll call of road kills in the sky.
Son, keep your armor shining.
Steal a few winks and you do.

GETTING AFTER OUR BOYS

Get tough now? Too late.
White hair's hanging down my neck.

Sure, five boys is all right!
but one with fire?

Billy Boy is two times eight
and unequalled for sloth.

Jimmy Boy promises and promises
to think.

Sam and Tom are thirteen
and don't know six plus seven.

Our hopeful is about nine
and would rather climb a tree.

—This is how heaven fills the world with weeds
and why the bottle with dad's drink.

—T'ao Ch'ien

THREE MEN IN A BOAT: MEXICO 1958

I.

To rustle up adventure we headed south, at Matamoros
reconsidered clear to Alaska, bought insurance
and passed over the border.

The three of us made our way to Acapulco to watch
the long fall of the deep-into-the-sea and live-to-dare divers
who leap as boys from lower rocks, climb higher
as their eye on the incoming wave sees keener.
They keep the tiempo of the sequential watery cushion far below,
dive and splash over rocks in a pool rising just deep
enough in the lifting wave.

On the evening beach fire comes out of your hand
when you slice the water of the Pacific, the great commensurate
of our first visit.

With a will we hired a sail to fish for marlin at dawn
the winds were searching a flag to tear.
Out farther it stilled.
Bottom fishing had brought sea bass and the handsome dogfish
off Myrtle Beach the summer before in gentle Captain Wheat's boat.
Those with bad-luck bellies had cast their lunches to the wind.
Here the Acapulco boat was private. Sharks came first.

These gents lay as if sleeping it off on deck
laid out in black tuxedo with foulard at the neck,
sartorial hit men for the blue marlin.
Theirs was never the only game in town unless you were swimming.

A sea turtle called by the port side
like a checker cab flag up looking for a fare.

———

Unlike a stiffening shark zipped in a tuxedo with a rifle shot in the head
it had an easy, round, dark green welcoming manner.

With no prelude Bayard jumped on the rail and sized up the angle
for a leap to its barnacled, lichen-soft back.
Breast bone smash against ridge of shell?
Let him leap. Isn't boy on a dolphin a Platonic Idea?
Cretan maid balanced on a bull's back? Shamu the killer whale
gives a ride to this little girl on her birthday.
Mortal and nature may be at one again.

Our man was gathered to accept the invitation.
The big fellow in the water off port was patient splashing.
What was the risk? A foot shorn off? A strong swimmer pulled below?
The morning before just off the beach schnorkling the underworld
when until air at the surface burst forth
the sudden marvel would not let me go.

So Bayard poised, we saboteurs scared or prudent, as duty-bound
as he to hold up the venture, we disappointeurs in the keep,
tangled up his legs and pulled him down. The bad angel in me,
the poor tipper, had won the moment. Fear or prudence
subtracted a story for generations.

Later back at the dock we caught Barney and his vertical ten-foot marlin
side-by-side in a silverado photo.

II

Innocence was ablaze in eyes looking on Pedro Vargas,
el Tenor Continental, that evening in Mexico City.
At our balcony table his singing blew away the old.

Ah, his voice made a lot of things easier to understand.
"Monasterio Santa Clara"—pure spun gold!
We vowed to make the pilgrimage.
In transport the audience lifted cheers to his bows.

Proving there is a divine sense of humor
the host at that moment seats Mr. Tex and his Doña
at our table of glamour where el Tenor chaired us to bliss.
"Call me Sagebrush, boys." Here is a conquistador with fun on his arm.
Wattles bang his bolo. His eye glows with the
pride and lust of a turkey. "I'm Sage and" (turning to the lady)
"this here's—." I swear he said Santa Clara herself.

She smiles and music is made flesh,
young, Latin, and full of grace.
Heavenly saints, lead me to the Communion Table.

Tribute in devotion was laid before her in a swirl of innocence
about that blessed table on the balcony. Only our eyes
spoke Spanish. Alas. Before Pedro rose to cry again
the turkey in the cowboy hat had begun to smoke from the ears.
As tight as a rattler he pulled out and laid on the table cloth
before us and all the world a six-shooter as if it were Exhibit A.

Oh it wasn't to be fired, but it wanted to be so oh
with breathless muzzle smokeless touch-me-trigger.
Forefinger pad, here's the place. Stroke the chamber.

Sage had flown his private plane South of the Border
to lay the ardor chiller on the cloth field before us,
two shavetail BAs and a BS out on Mexico City.
If I'd known Spanish. . . . But a dead man tells no tales.
The old coot wasn't the only chicken at table.

In my sly heart I toasted her quickest widowhood.

Below to the band the couples dance a ballroom of sails.
Pedro Vargas the Dark Pope is singing the club into a cathedral.
In this shadow play the tinkle of holy music is a lessoning,
a spot of tiempo. Home in your northern retreat show may trap you
under the cellar door with your would-have-been loves
like powder suddenly on your shoulder.
Without fair warning a chill of song falls upon your hair again.

III

At the bullfight the matador can't place the coup de grâce
on the last bull. Spectators push into the arena
to throw seat cushions over the horned one, the fighter
who's standing foursquare and bullish.
Bright colors rise against his shining flanks.

Aside with the sword swears one marginalized matador.
In provincial rings in Spain dwarf matadores cómicos
dedicated to the blood sport intend this effect.

BALLAD OF THE BELLES

In the washed air of the Spring Festival
beauties line in the bank of the lake in our capital Long Peace.
Their dress is rich, their minds lofty.
Their skin is smooth, their fingers elegant.
Gold peacocks and silver unicorns glow
on their embroidered spring gowns.
Their hair? Ah, coiffed clouds spin.
Around the middle? Nets of pearl flush the waist.
The titled ladies of the duchies Kuo and Ch'in
have floated to us from spice-veiled chambers.

From green tureens the banquet camel roasts
rise in purple humps.
Yet the noses of the rhino chopsticks
are loath to sniff the dishes.
For naught the belled scimitars
carve the air with jingles,
though the flying bridles of the eunuchs
raise no dust
as royal kitchens parade the Eight Tastes.

Come first ancient flutes and drums that
  now will quake ghosts and gods.
Oh, how leisurely he ambles his dallying mount
  to the pavillion,
how he dismounts the brocade carpet.
Announce milord Willow Down, who will fling his snow
over the frogbits of our dark floating ponds.
Looping a shadow of bluebird in streams
  an arrow of red in her beak:
  milady's handkerchief.

———

When this lord blazes, you can warm your hands.
A moment! One caution: don't let his eyes open on you.

—Tu Fu

THE MOUNTAINS

LIFT UP MINE HILLS

The dropping road makes spit-out-of-the-window quick
turns down to a valley abandoned under a cliff.
We have come to the mountains for a start up

the road back, to be made whole after blindness.
I shout to all who can hear, I've forgotten I was blind.
As a boy I ran, but after, I lay inside.

The sudden meadow surprises us in its high comfort.
On the ridge against clouds and sky
the blue trees have been caught naked.

This must be the valley we came from,
landlocked for generations. In dreams when she appears
we go to the clay bank off Rivermont Avenue

now behind the Church of Christ Scientist.
Sycamores are up and down by every creek,
elms long before the blight, dogwoods, hickories.

Mother and boy make bowls with their hands
to trick the water to stay.
The muddy traveler from the locked mountain

which once was silver has come a long way.
I will know how it has to go
on down between the orange banks

under the high heads of trees
which have left us gracious space.
How can silver be blind and see?

———

Be bare water yet dark?
Shut your eyes
and you may sit beside her.

She signaled, she was the presence.
While she sat on top of the bank,
she must have remembered.

THE ORNAMENTAL ZITHER

Why are there fifty strings on the brocaded zither?
No answer.
Each string, each bridge
counts a lost year.

Chuang Tzu wanders on
in a waking dream of butterflies.
With every cuckoo's summer cry
Emperor Wang bleeds in shame and lust.

Over cold oceans the moon still flushes pearls to tears.
The sun still warms jade to smoke
on Indigo Mountain.

How could that moment become a remembrance past
when, tranced,
it only happened as a memory?

—Li Shang-yin

THERE'S NO ROAD IN

People are asking the way to cold mountain.
Cold mountain. There's no road in.
Summers the ice won't let go.
When a sun comes out, it's the fog's magic show.

How could following me get you there?
My bearings aren't your bearings.
If Your Honor chimed in with me,
you'd arrive heart-center.

—Han Shan

AFTER RETURNING FROM THE MOUNTAINS
OCTOBER 12TH WHEN WE PLAYED W & L IN FOOTBALL

Again, why in the do I live flatlands?
Up on Big Spy Lookout we turned and turned around 360 degrees
of mountains backed up by more even in the light rain.
Conclusion: "—must live here."

Just out of sight of Big Spy up a lane still thick with purple
rested South Mountain Cemetery and Chapel on the slanted hillside.
"Born to bud on Earth and bloom in Heaven." "Gone but not For-
gotten."
But the headstone whose forgotten words I sought from the last visit
              was gone.

Back at the sign the road to the left takes you to Nelson County
to the apple orchards. Down at Massies Mill the mud mark might still
show over the doors from the burst river in the seventies.
We took the right and curved to Vesuvius north of Lexington.

Off the mountain we drove faster and came up behind a pickup
whose bumper sticker read: "My Jesus was a Jewish carpenter."
Almost rear-ended to make out the message on the mud flaps:
Misty, misty? Hasty, hasty?
Twins in stereo. Aha! "Nasty, nasty," they kicked as we passed,

shooting a look at the driver,
"Nasty, nasty."

Except Nelson County and these pictures all
were taken last Saturday before the game this October fall,
not the summer at the sheriff's cabin when I ran
under the oak-exploded birds

to the brimming urn in another country graveyard
that never dry refilled itself, spilling measures over its lip.
Unconscious the landlady's horse came up behind in the still pasture
and nuzzled my neck.

BURLESQUE BUDAPEST

THE RE-CREMATION OF SAM MCGEE

Thermals, union suit, long johns,
you bet I got mine on:

on and off in November
and on steady into December

for three and a half months.
Cut them off with scissors once

it's springtime,
like slicing off the rind

of a ripe wedge of cheese,
the only way to beat this baltic freeze

of my feet and toes,
two hoary, half-froze

slabs of bacon just dying
to be frying

in a red-hot black skillet.
That'll do it, or will it?

CHARLIE THE CHAPLIN AND THE LAND OF LIBERTY

By twenty-six the most highly paid actor in the world
he'd learned the backward
kick. From dice in steerage, the preca-
rious dignity of the Alas-
ka Jump, the Louisiana Purchase, the hang
together or a part
he'd dream up on the spot.

Some survivals are a success.
His begins in Keystone anarchy
on the same page as the forgotten etymology
of chaplain (an uncle weak in spelling).
Charlie Chaplain was Johnny Chapman was
Appleseed strolling seeds and trees
from the ground up
all the way through Indiana.
Under eyebrows he was full of beans by the knifeful
in every farmwife's kitchen.

So the back kick, success,
Charlie never lies, our Seward's Folly. Grip
with your toes or your soles, any kid
might make it all the way to Nome.
He can haul up his galluses and fly like an angel.
Spending the shutter he wins improvisatore,
disappears down any road with hat and cane,
any man's mustache, luck.

SHOT ON THE RADIOACTIVE SET:
OUR COUNTDOWN WITH THE DUKE

With the sparkle in Sam's hair this morning
the year flicked on spring

as we rose to sing in sun motes
and called back a recent Academy Award,

the Duke's last hurrah. He carried it off
with the reassuring rattle in his throat.

This place isn't big enough for many
Methuselahs, he intimated.

If you say that
you won't be all wrong.

Heroes who ride all day and shoot
the laconic Colt

take their stand with litotes,
even though the fire inside

is spreading.
Who could have thought the desert wasn't free,

and the painted hills beyond politics?
Caution. These days your lookout

might turn out to be out anybody's dacha,
even with your guard up and your partner riding shotgun.

Western water leaps from the living spring?
It might be the enemy that hands you the canteen.

But, though mustered out, he's still
royalty of the celluloid,

still the dusty duke.
We're waiting together. It's high noon.

We're standing at the bar.
Somebody's pushing through the swinging doors

we should have killed a long time ago.
We'll take him out.

In the deep saloon our ready bones
burn like neon tubes inside our Levi's,

our alert heads
glow through Stetsons like eggs.

LUCAN'S DEATH

In my tub I recite the select death of Cato's Tullus
to give me one final spit from the Wars.
Pompey's soldiers lie again on the gorgonized desert

among strange serpents. Iuvenus magnanimus is stung by the blood-rheum
and spouts (for his theater carmen) saffron-water
out of a hundred lips sliced in the metal statue.

Would you not pick your lines of exit?
I, Lucan, sing in my Stoic tub
of haemorrhois of the squamose coils.

For the Emperor he knew well, otiose Antium's son
(a town long thinned of pirate's blood),
and where he was a pain.

A.D. 65, Lucan twenty-six, silenced, mutinous,
Nero, who'd two years longer to do his work,
by then a kinsman, wife, and mother under belt,

had fiddled Rome's distraction
and blamed the burning on the Christians.
He allowed Lucan to choose his poison,

who also picked the text for the event.
From the word of the desert crossing
and lines that stretched out the Libyan tribe that scaled and smoked

and spewed and stank, he matched the man.
Aptest? Over prester, seps, dipsas, chersydros and chelydrus
he passed, over those of lisped names

———

all spawned as Medusa drooped her head
to clot of gore and Libyan dirt the deathliest tribe of serpents,
and chose haemorrhois.

True, like Perseus he must have quivered over amphisbaena,
whose twin heads misdirected are two mouths
to bite at either end, oral yet anal,

the limbless lizard deaf and blind
of two trunks pulling north and south.
What better emperor of death?

Nero incarnate! But the cousin touched the heart,
not just the mind, and Lucan sinking in the stoic tub
picks haemorrhois of the squamose coils.

So he sings his echo. A farewell has been cut:
son of Cordova (known for her leather), harpied by gorgon-spawn,
I told of wars too well.

NEW WORLD ENTERTAINMENT
AT BURLESQUE BUDAPEST

A high school tour from Stamford, CT, to Eastern Europe
has been kept off the streets at night and treated to
a diverting show within the hotel, in which, contesting
desire and satiety, obeying higher laws of space and time,
the fancy guys and gals begin buck naked
and to the tune of the New World Symphony draw on sensual
threads up to earmuffs and overalls.

I, clothed, sing of naked by whom and why
Chris the Cave Man is my source.

Here on the stage are the facts
as they were told me, reduced to our size

for all the world to see
as bare and ruddy as a baby's toe.

New Englanders ever voyaging out,
the class tour to Europe's walls

was kept off the boulevards and byways of Budapest
and treated to the hotel's won first-night in-house show

(until you find your sea legs). Hurrah
the hotels' own, which includes a modest, thoughtful native strip

for American guests to our city.
It's called the paprika-put-it-on and the tunes are whistled Dvořák.

Now there're as many kinds of BUR-L-E-Q as BARB-B-Q
but the usual way is universal, I'm told.

———

Up on the stage body wraps are unwrapped, toyed with,
and tossed in the muzzle of the paying crowd, who bays.

The object is to make the birthday suit
as interesting as possible when it finally appears.

Delay is important.
Toys may figure in the game.

But the dancers of Budapest had rethought the business
and began buck naked.

Naked as a tooth they bounded over the boards
without a shoe, comb, or pasty on their dimpled bodies,

for the show was their enrobement itself.
They put it on the same direction the band from Stamford

once they've caught their breath, which had left,
put their eyes back in. The drift of the tale is now well known in CT.

They pulled on twill by twill
to the music *From the New World*.

The tune began with simple twat and Dvořák
then threw melodious silk up the legs over the eggs

as the sea salt rises over the slick hull,
which smacked with a champagne bottle hung on a rope

slides down the slip into the wash
and floats away.

All of which poses as romance intercontinental.
Then the artists reached the finale—

every great attention must grow slack—
of fur burns and ear flaps and the ultimate overcoat.

Were they just cold?
Cavie didn't say the season.

We cheered the bumps and grinds in great coats
before our broad-minded, democratic eye.

Maybe we'd stumbled into a fashion show where weeds are the thrill,
the buff to start smoothly untextiled.

Or into chef's school where tasting backwards
begins a banquet with solid dessert?

True, we are all let raw, ready or not,
beautiful more or less,

out of mama's legs at birth. But these proleptic
performers in Budapest on the Danube

began as bare as a baby's bumbo and to Dvořák, Bartók
dressed up into garb as if into a higher state.

The decorums of space and time will never be the same
in Connecticut or wherever the Cave Man sings.

WAR FEVER

WAR FEVER

War engines can start like an ordinary lawnmower kicks up.
Last summer a boy in Charlotte was killed cutting the grass.
But that was after a rain and in high grass,
electrocuted, not run on gas.

Or war engines can begin like feathers:
hear the flying tigers whir? Or sound like a cap pistol
when somebody to be famous leans back in the limousine and gives up.

Or the tick of harness as it lifts something into heavy position,
like a little girl examining medals
or a mother resting in a rocking chair.

The sound of waiting? No. Waiting weighs a ton
but it never started anything
until it was over. The ticking of synchronized watches
can just mean guarded borders.

You know how winding down sounds too: patience wearing out
like old teeth.
Grandfather's uniforms leap in the closet with a clatter.

PEACH ORCHARDS UP I-85
AFTER THE PRESIDENT'S SPEECH ON THE DRAFT

Interstate 85 crosses that combed order of rolling winter orchards
like a cicatrix, row by fast row that care has pruned the slough
to rest for sun, the rush of blossom, the long lying in for the
full season of fruit.

Shaner's son once drove our crowd in an open Ford bounding
like a loosed terrier
through like lines of orchard trees, but those were wilder apple,
a catalogue of acres Delicious, Stayman Winesap, Red Astrakhan,
Northern Spy, Delicious,

up and down the row beds where one sprays summers or
sets out pots to burn in cold.
Old Shaner'd planted peaches first, and spring after had dreaded,
trembled over the dread frost. That climate would give any
soul of peach the brows.

That was farther north of here but south of son. Driven from the field
he lay bedfast for days until his spring brows stopped jumping
like Uncle Ben's mouth, gassed in the War, sucking
on his pipe in gulps,

never enough air to breathe since the Marne. Shaner's nerves
are quiet now
like his buried orchard of peaches, the trees he, quit, slew and burnt.
So his son talked family, drove us up and down, named apples,
smoked convertible cigars that put us in mind of frost pots
a chilling April.

That was summer, that open, bounding ride. Today shows no
signs of a crashing roadster,

no signs of even smoke stealing through
the orchard cold far from Arlington.

Minded, cropped heads ordered elsewhere lay down their sacrifice,
a twilight season which will be long,
who wonder why flowers and the hanging of stone fruit
never come.

THE BALLAD OF THE ARMY WAGONS

Wagons bump, bump, horses neigh, neigh,
Soldiering men, bow and arrow are at each waist.
Mothers, fathers, wives, children force their way alongside
  to see them off.
All-Sun Bridge is invisible in the dust.
Grabbing at clothes, stamping feet, jammed together,
weeping, the weeping reaches high heaven.

A passer-by calls to the soldiers.
The soldiers just say,
                "The drafting keeps on and on.
Some of us went north at fifteen to guard the River,
now at forty we go to camps in the West.
Going, the mayor wrapped our turbans for us,
coming home gray-headed, we turn around again
  for the frontier.
At the frontier the blood fills an ocean.

" 'The Warrior Emperor Opens the Territories!'
Sir, you haven't heard that in the lands of Han
  east of the mountains
a thousand villages and ten thousand crossroads
  grow briars?
A strong wife can hoe and plough,
the crops still sprout everywhere with no east
  or west to rows.
It's worse for the tough fighters from Ch'in.
They round them up like dogs or chickens.

"Thank you, but what can we say against the state?
See, this winter the West-of-the-Pass Division is
  still fighting.

The tax man wants more, from what we don't know.
Yes, we know to have sons is bad.
No, it is better to have daughters.
They grow up and marry the neighbor.
Sons, their bones will lie in lost grasses.

"Sir, do you know that on the shore of Blue Sea
no one has gathered the white bones for years?
New ghosts, cheated, are vexed. Old ghosts weep.
When the heavens grow sullen and rain sheets down,
you can hear. They cheep like birds and insects."

—Tu Fu

REMEMBERING RED CLIFF GONE BY

to the tune of "The Charms of Nien-nu"

The great river runs eastward,
ever sifting away the dashing fighters of the past.
West of the ancient ramparts it's still said
once was the Red Cliff of Childe Chou
  of the Three Kingdoms.
Shattered rocks scarp the air,
startled waves crack agains the banks
and roll up a thousand snow drifts.
The river and the cliff are like a painting:
a single season of how many heroes?

From far away my mind invokes Duke Chou,
just wed to the younger of the lovely Ch'iao sisters.
He was a worthy of wit and deed.
Before his father fan, silken turban, his chat
  and easy laughter,
the ashes of the strong foe flew, the smoke vanished.
So into the ancient kingdom my spirit roams.
The tender heart must laugh,
me, my hair growing gray early.
Our life is like a dream.
One cupful I'll pour out to the watery moon.

—Su of the Eastern Slope

DARWIN DOUBTS THE MIAMI RIOTS

Neanderthal the bigger brain,
and ours is marching toward the prune?

Nonsense. Aghast? Listen to the stomp in the street.
When I read the paper my feet

dance. With the Herald my stomach kicks. Tribune
says my man inside wants his

Miami and his man's eyes
and tongue off the street on a skewer.

Did Grandfather brew a bigger pit
of blood than this? Grin to watch it

boil off into stones in the belly
of the kettle?

Teeth can be as fine as the edge of a collar.
Grandmother's back is patient as crochet.

In the woman's lodge of cicatrix
there're always flowers.

Did Grandma pull a fine, tight stitch
by iron box of fire or

by a pit in Aurora's clay mouth?
She'd say, the sunrise mornings

is anybody's cave on Flagler.
Aye, upright, you're proud your tail may fade

———

and second stomach dwindle
to a finger.

But fooled, any smarter set of ears may sprout.
Consider your higher hands

thicken daily with cuff link and cravat,
ancestral knot,

numble the esteemed mutt's tightening collar.
Note on the Beach how the gift of thumbs fumbles

with tiny catches of sunglasses.
Let's walk our way back

from the billiard's click
through the streets of this city

where the colors preen.
The screw and the fulcrum, the wheel

and the lever, note where we leave each behind.
Here we can drop all the pulleys in the sea,

soon talk to the sun long before Liberty fell,
and the end of the Tamiami Trail.

For now, cast a trout line out the window
into the painted lane

whose apricot and peach
pick up the sun

through any May's volcanic gloom.
Rainbows leap

between the floating buildings
and bells ring holy over rising Everglades.

NYC MARATHON NOVEMBER 4TH

In memory of Bill Hight, who did not suffer
fakes gladly but endured them, knowing us for
what we were.

So you want to be inclusive? Join the marathon club
(the body wasn't meant to stand that treatment)
or watch, November 4th, Central Park, "BE HAPPY JUST SMILE,"
where yesterday a citizen in a message cap planted by the path talked to
autumn trees as ragged as be, a salute to colors.

The day's of the trumpet and alarm against fenced
cities and against high towers. They're pounding by,
terrorists running the marathon
the heart was no more meant to withstand
than brains to sizzle in a pan.
25,000 canter through world famous potholes
cast in plaster to try the Japanese axle.

A legless man dribbles on his knuckles, wheelchairs fly.
They also serve who stand and wait
for the athletes to pass.
They also serve who only buy a T-shirt.
Buy a burger, float a balloon, light and lively.
Careless Bob Coulibri jumped
the ropes without a number, dodging officials
did not stop him.
TAKE A BITE OF LIFE.

Onward rose the ten thousands through canyons and well
wishers. If bridges are arcs and spans Bob on a numberless
stopped and posed with Euclid geometrically peed
over and out of sight off the Verrazano-Narrows Bridge.
Not a bum's waste in a corner.

Stop, poseur! Stop, poseur!
That's a free, unstopped marathon pee beyond recognition.

"Live in my heart
rent-free."
But watch out for the worm in the bagel.

"The secret is to keep moving in this city."
See up. In the high red steel

the acro-enzyme-deficient walk surely across
crossties into the masthead.
They are free of further falls and build above.
The secret to keep is moving in this city.

South of Houston St. in graceful cast-iron design
welkin-eyed SoHo artists have lived in lofts
with enough room for the lungs.
There they've built their art for a time.

But beware the copycats. Beware the galley-crawlers in top coats
who cop the cheese and importune the speaker. Beware pickpockets.
In the O. K. galleries buildings glow in the dark
and the security man is utterly unflappable.
Walk on eggshells. If you seek air, give the room lungs.
For behind subsequent copycats follow and throw up walls of sham.
"How can you tell a true cast-iron building from the counterfeit?"
"Hold a magnet against the suspect and see whether it sticks."
Ladies and gentlemen, the ceiling far above your heads
is gold leaf, maintenance-free.

———

If you've left your A. K. D. behind
you're in as much trouble in N. Y. C.
as in DA. C. academic circles within circles.
Bereft of the Automatik Krap Detektor
you're buzzard meat on either Kampus.
The officious Panda of Asian games stands Square,
"with his great bland countenance, as if for the world to worship."
Fellow monads, our antipodes, the costumes were already built.

Hard, scouts! You've been looking in the wrong place.
Take a bite out of life, chew it.
Behind the scrim lit runners charge at us
cut off at the shoulders then drop down the reserve rakes stage
bob about the curved path by the crowds into Central Park south.
Shouts fill the trees behind the iron paling.
We buy a T-shirt for the day to fight cancer.
"And their blood shall pour out as dust
and their flesh as the dung."

"Keep moving" was John's advice to swim in the city
above whose park from the Athletic Club we watched the colors.
There's always change. Some buildings are now cylinders,

Marty pointed, not old New York City boxy.
Can a building become a tree?
Herb tells students to fail.
Little Tree talks to oaks and dreams of ghosts in cherry trees past.

Impossible to talk to this place in all its languages.
If you believe in grammar you believe in God.
Dogs we dyslectics believe in who know their master's voice.
The devil speaks all tongues with a tall-tail accent.

Emerson built the New World on solid proverbs.
"To tell people each other's names
when they meet for the first time" defines introduction.

Easy, night scouts after the show, stare too hard
and miss the center of the star.
Just watch the dim crosstown streets.
FIRE FEEDS ON CARELESS DEEDS.
At the keyboard of the delayed reaction organ
one keeps half a note ahead.
Only the principal tenor can always open the window.
Far below the underground where the Phantom plays
the diggers strike water.

Over on our left there the street people of the avenue have retired
like rugs rolled up to the dark wall.
They warm the foot of the building
which is the silenced recycling center at Columbus Circle.
One mummy sleeps like a body bagged head to heel—
one dog tag prized between teeth, the second looped about the big toe?
My, two oversized, alien bagels are left on a plate for the morrow.
They're eaten now unless he still sleeps.
They were not stolen to tell you this.
The tailor and the seamstress do distress an operatic costume.

Home again, what was the battle? what campaign? which war?
Both Coulibris are elsewhere seeking authenticity.
It was all part of the broken marathon November 4th in the city.
                    —with a tip of the hat to
                        The Book of Zephaniah,
                        The Gray Goose Press,
                        Cockburn's Millennium,
                        and *Fodor's New York*

AN OLD SOCCER PROPHET WAKES UP
IN MECKLENBURG RED CLAY, FALL 1992

The game has begun. Our kicks are smart, even artistic, thunderous.
The enemy rolls about caught in the net like vicious squirrels.
Pindar, where are you to celebrate this leap and pass?
These are the truly pointy heads and toes.

The enemy is opposite, may their keeper suffer the fate of no divine saves.
Ours has made those.
May their kickers score own goals. May their tricks be ours.
May our defenders deny them salvation unless they cry uncle.

When we close in, may their keeper enjoy
a digestion of scores in the mouth and arms.
May our attackers uncork a cannon ball into their net
and discombobulate their reins.

May our red clay stick to their bones.

DOLPHINS IN OUR WOODS

CNUT'S SONG
for Astri

The scrap of first English
by casual accident
lies here before you in this book.

I saw the blue eye of a three-year-old
touch its first jay
over the fall field in a scrub pine.

The king rested in the boat
as the rowers pulled closer
to the monks' merry song.

JUNE DUSK

You realized the same moment
a rabbit's ears were lettuce too
(that tail is cotton)
his nose like pajamas
and his feet like papa's slippers.

Or like snow shows
which are hands to run over snow.
Snow? she asked. June dusk in the backyard.
Though she was three winters old and knew the element
like me she had forgotten.

RAINY DAY

Mrs. Pierce shines four storm windows,
leans them on the front porch.

A passerby pauses to send a stone through each
and stumble on through myriads of starfish and sand dollars

splashing about his feet.
The flood is sure to come.

On the Carolina coast rain blurs pelicans
swallowing their laughter.

In the Piedmont woods take the water.
Outside our window a flicker affronts

the slick pine claw-held,
and there by the front walk

if you came for a visit you would pass
one week's dissolving possum.

So much water in one possum.
A shoe is by the gate filling.

Three children at panes guess the rain.
No dolphins in our woods.

IT'S FALL AGAIN

It's fall again. Leaves
flee the slow trees
and run in the new September wind.
Farther south hurricanes blow
water over the boots of bitten shores.
In the north the devil is making ready
to deliver snow as beautiful as bones.
The heads of trees and buildings march
stone bodies in the retreat.
A fire truck cruises by broadcasting
      all you can eat
              fish fry
                  fry.
The fish lie burnt on the trenchers
like fried fingers.
Old men under grey hats lean chairs to brick,
adjust boots on rung, spit,
and watch the parade.

NEW SNOW

The new snow on old pine needles
was like the latest newspaper photograph of leukemia.
I stopped to hear something beside myself,
bear in raincoat by cast in the tire track
giving all the evidence they needed,
pointed as it was up the piney path.
An edge of sound was all,
kept out of the drama.
Ah, but I sensed
(dirty up by the side of the road)
it had snowed into drifts:
too cold there to melt
—a spell in the Caribbean? write your next book in
   Hawaii??
Snow tramps have a place in the heel
that will never thaw until
like Shelley's the body burns twice
and they bury the heart too briny to burn.
Rage against autumn was disarmed by this breakfast
   snow,
barn at seven, breath like a horse's.
When I left the needles were still in the path;
now afternoon it blows
up from the ground into the trees.

SPRING DECEMBER

old man winter in the salon
plays before the window.
out comes cold Chopin

December first is a spring day
the birds who remained cry spring songs
and the trees sweat in anticipation

but the gentleman playing
can only pay in snow.
though his face is warm in the breeze
he can only speak and pay in snow

bees today who work
soon see their honey frozen in wax.
he concentrates on the music
quite wasted in the garden.

POCAHONTAS AND THE DRUNKEN WAITER

he walked down the road holding a platter of air
the glasses bobbed like corks
and a naked pearl fisher swam by his ear
he said: lord protect me from myself

God held a funnel over the platter
and like beer poured over a cubic mile of air
he walked in haste and said:
I have twenty-eight glasses plus the holy chalice
god help me

a tree reached for him like seaweed
and a cow puckered a goldfish kiss
lord save me from myself he groaned
and looked for a goal

out of the corn rushed Indian maidens
and stuck his skin with feathers
love love love they cried
save me

he pitched the platter
and popped his eyes at their black buttons
as these ghosts laid him with a fish
under the silky corn

HER FIRST LATIN: A PRAYER

After the first lessons the first accusative: the tree
gives a branch to swing on. May it never be
a spear for friend or enemy.

Puellae portant aquam.
They pause, drink: I understand.
Never so cool before. Novam amant agricolae terram.
The farmers are tilling in invisible hills.

Do the parsing hours sow seed or salt?
Such is fifty years their freight.
You will know the words for what you do.
Speak and be rid of the poison. Odi et amo.

May you never need some:
hot wind over the roof, the child as still as a cold storm in his arms.
The tufted egret
is grotesque.

Nay, may your language be,
though the marsh green is different one year, the tree
lends a branch to swing on.
Agricolae amant terram, puellae portant aquam.

FIRST GRADE

our boy said SH is a sound
                              a ship makes
          and CH a train moving
he was learning sounds and letters
on this gusty autumn day of leaves
          and rushing trees.

ACROSTIC

Four-year-old Shaw
Opened up the conversation with Bestepappa
Under the pecan tree: "I
"Remember being born out of Mamma's throat."
"You what? You remember that
"Early? Amazing, Shaw!"
"And before I was born I knew the name of eve-
"Rybody in the w-
"Orld." We were eating our bag
Lunches and
Discussing life
Sixty-four years apart three years ago.
He added yesterday, "Our gym te-
"Acher told us, 'You're always balancing," he stood on one foot, 'even
" 'when you're eating at the table or fast asleep in bed.'"

WHATEVER THAT DONKEY IS
for Siri Lise and Robb, August 18th

Dad reties my bowtie and props up the shower
in my tux pocket. The blower's on the hip at the ready.
Mother's at my side smiling I believe.

This is about sweetness and light.
There's a corsage to be proffered.
A bit of powder's in the air.

Love may or may not find you a pal,
but by heavens this is oxygen I breathe.
Then there's the matter of luck,

whatever that donkey is,
and you're picking out bridesmaids' dresses
with your daughter.

The balloons in the sky don't care a strawberry
who sent them up. Don't sneeze
or it's cupid's quick arrow into the hide.

Pick out the colors
and the wind may bring you a blimp.
That's love.

I'm as certain as the breeze is
where the next dirigible will lightly crash
or call if you will ride.

PLOPS

to the tune of "The Lotus-Gatherers' Song"

Water chestnuts wave in the ripples, the lotus moves in
  the wind.

Where the lotus flowers are thick, a little boat pushes
  through.

She is meeting her young gentleman, wants to talk, drops
  her head, grins.

Then she scratches her head, and a nice piece of green
  jade falls off in the water.

—Po Chü-I

A PIECE OF JADE AND CHANCE'S MAN

In the woods you can find a dead doe.
Wrap her in plain rushes.
She was dreaming in the spring sun
When chance's man whispered in her ear.

In the woods you can find a dead deer.
Use white rushes to shroud her.
Some girls are like a piece of jade.
In among the trees open paths and close in the underbrush.

Careful! Please!
Don't pull my sash.
Don't make the dogs bark.

—The Book of Songs,
Folk Song No. 23

BIRD AND BUGSONG IS ACTIVE EARLY
for Siri Lise and Robb

A hideaway not quite underground to work after dinner,
in the basement study the window is one porthole of a row
just above the waves of the garden. A bush kept out by the sliding window
splashes against my nose. By the far stream a low dog leaps.
Apple and pear trees take up most of the sky.

But I'm hard at work, and the pipes are singing.
All's almost right with the world. Out there somewhere
the water's on and it's green. I pen the words louche of eye,
broken of lip. It's a Byronic patch, surely

not the last tonight. A studied pause follows.
Ho! The glass crashes with thrumming.
A tropical storm at the window!
Not made to take a beating. Hold up!

Water drums on the blind, simple pane.
Thank the heavens closed. Then the pounding stills as quick.
Through the streaming glass my bride stands blurred,
knee-deep in green. Her wet face wears a wide-angled grin.

Once upon a morning, bent over a rosebush right where she stands,
caught off guard, I jumped to hear Mormor call good morning.
Not tired? Not still sleeping after her trip from Norway, in the basement
where the sun comes slow and late to the low side of the house?

The bird and bugsong is active early.
The road has built up with houses farther out, but we're still country.
In years that surprise may have been about halfway
between our vow and yours in the spring.
She's always brought a blessing with her visit.

WEDDING RECEPTION ON THE OSLO FJORD

Oh the laughter of you ladies-in-waiting al fresco
with the gentlemen attendant beside you tuxedo'd!

May your shoulders long magic my memory.
Under flags through the fjord there glimmering

the teak hull swanlike hauls a slowly silvered
wake which rolls a bright train in a mirror

of dizzy clouds who've forgotten the lost hour
of sleep. Out step the bride and the groom in a shower

of hip hip hurrahs while flowers O you flowers dance
by the white night shore of the tide entranced.

I stand swept by the wide water's quiet
brimming. Far out the shell of one kayak
draws a long salute to the pageant.

A MEDITATION ON THE OSLO FJORD ATTEMPTED IN THE MANNER OF ODD NERDRUM

Water? Think of water? The Oslo fjord.
I fall into the icy Oslo fjord.

I see a man afloat by the wet rocks
just there where the Naesodden ferry docks

a half-hour's sail from Oslo City Hall,
whose twin towers rise stark brick red and tall

against the town. O'er all rises the white
ski jump that commands the hills. In the bright

fall sun amidst this splendid north he floats,
while back and forth to Oslo ply the boats.

He looks like Charlie Chaplin bobbing black
in soggy coat and baggy pants, the back

of his head hidden by his bowler, arms
outstretched and void, bereft of all his charms.

This face has been looking at the bottom
of the fjord for a long time, as forgotten

as drowned men must feel. The swells that lift, lower
him have all the time in the world and more.

Someone in crouched position leans out far
with a wet pole to mosey him ashore.

The body dances free. "Why bother us?
"You cannot bring him back to life or trust.

"So let us have our play." I ken the words.
The legs of the man with the pole grow tired.

He straightens up to give his bones relief.
Three seabirds skim and dart above the deep.

He rears and hurls at them a polar roar
over the steady flood of the old fjord
about her islands and against her shore,

then pauses, takes a moment, shakes one soggy
trouser leg, and then the other loggy

with cold, black fjord water. He will restore
the blood of life to the man stretched out sore
and broken on Naesodden's shore.

HOW DO WE CAPTURE A DROWNED BODY?
OR, THE USE OF DOUBLE NETS

In Oslo's fjord some years ago
we saw our first—at least 'twas so
for me—amazingly vivid
on that cold summer day Næsod-
den-bound, just off the ferry to
the great peninsula, the wet-through
brown back that bobbed like a whale's back
but didn't spout,
                the hat that sat
tight upon the submerged head must
have been
           knotted under the chin
a shoe broke the surface now and then
the ferryman gave a shout

"Get him out!"

"Hjelp! Hjelp!" Then there appeared out
of nowhere an overlong stick
with nets of rope at both ends fit
for double duty to dip, cup
a drowned and soggy body up
from Oslo's fjord as the ferry
struck out for Næsodden carrying
our party and the man who
                wouldn't tonight start his dinner with the soup
dish.

HOIST A SAIL

NEW YEAR'S BIRTHDAY
for S.

The gravel truck drove into our sky this evening
And dumped out diamonds.
The heavens have become a precious field.

Winter birthdays are like that,
beards fly and the breath glows—
spring will flush her favor in the new woods

but winter has his open poplars and high air.
Deep summer has her ardor
but winter grinning firedogs and fire in goblets.

I would give you
a pride of Chinese kites over our house,
a white tiger and a floating golden phoenix.

The new year begins on your ninth.
Hoist a sail above the roof
And we'll glide away in our secret boat.

MEMORY OF WHITE GARDENS
OSLO, 27.12.91

We must shake some sense into this white garden.
4 a.m. outside the hybel window a snowplow scoots
over insomnia forth and back.

Get up, back. Loves lie away from us.
I am hostage to insomnia
who cannot melt,

paid overtime for time and over, not want.
You, my dear, sleep on. The operator of the snowplow runs the pile up.
He has a warm bed left.

"It has been a wonderful Christmas. Another memory."
This Christmas. May I put a word in
the pajama pocket over the breast

of the soul towards whom mine
(another memory?)
inclines in her addition?

HONEYMOON

to the tune of "Fresh Chrysanthemums"

Pausing as she pulls the perfumed drapes
she teases with sweet nothings,
knits her exquisite eyebrows, pouts:
"The night will be so short!"

To warm the nuptials of the mandarin quilt
  (two holes for two heads)
she hastens the young bridegroom to bed first.
It isn't long before she forsakes her bit of needlework
and glides out of her gauzy drawers.
She gives herself to easy labors, long abandon.
  "Leave the lamp lit by the bed curtains
so I can look at your pretty face from time to time."

—Liu Yung

ROLL THE STONE AWAY

A FRIEND'S PAINTING
for D.C.H.

You can count the colors and inch the sides,
cut the golden section, weigh the hue, soak, and shine,
but don't like many miss the high face
stretched like the artist as a young man by a clock
or sitting by a heavy river in the Majorca year. Stay longer.

This man opens color as careful as a robin's egg.
The reds console stained glass,
the white's a dog's tooth.
His angels are as blue as a Madonna.
St. Mark's coveys are holy ghosts.

He is hardly still enough to paint.
Eyes pan two dimensions of brick
or a dropping tree of birds
and the hands have purpled the canvas.
His neck is swept with wings.

I made him sell his self-portrait,
the blackest bright pigments and sunniest saturnine ever seen
since Vincent burnt his hair red. Then I waited.
One night it became a vision. Silent colors hawked.
Everything is all right! All is solved!
I thought so. It was that quiet.

TWO LUTES AND A RECORDER

LAKE YI

Someone is playing a recorder, and you are in a boat
crossing to the beach there.
This evening we are sending you off.

On the lake, with one turn of your head,
the mountains turn green and roll the white clouds
           into scrolls.

HUT IN THE BAMBOO

Sitting along in the bamboo grove
I pick the zither and whistle along.

These are deep woods no one knows about.
A clear moon comes out and we shine at each other.

IN REPLY TO CHIEFTAIN CHANG

These evening years I like things quiet.
The dusty world didn't have much to do with the heart.
As for looking out for number one,
   I never worked out an agenda.
There is nothing grand about knowing the way home now.
In the pines the breeze cools me in my open-necked shirt.
The moon over the mountains silvers
   the lute I pluck.
You, sir, ask of honorable retirement?
Can you hear the song of the fisherman?
   It reaches deep inland.

—Wang Wei

WINE POEM NO. 1

The traffic where I built is terrible
but I don't hear a thing, not a cart or a horse.

You ask me how that can be?
When the heart is far away, nobody is at home.

I pick never-die mums by the hedge to the east
and keep an eye on South Mountain.

At dusk its mountain air makes me promises.
Birds flock in homeward flight.

There was something true in all of this,
but when I started to explain, I'd already lost the words.

—T'ao Ch'ien

REMEMBERING THE ONE AND ONLY C. SHAW SMITH,
WHO ENTERTAINED THE TROOPS
IN CHINA IN WORLD WAR II
AND ONCE UPON A STAGE
CHINA'S MAGICIAN LONG TACK SAM

It's as yesterday.
When you get there, look for old-timers, you say,
who saw Long Tack Sam's act with the goldfish bowl.
Some remember.
Then you opened the silk curtains and showed me.
I've watched his mastery in the theater of the mind ever since.
That was fall of '88 standing at the north end of Chambers Building
where as a student you'd played basketball in a vanished gym,
before we blew away to China.

Long Tack Sam—poised there raises empty hands
to the hush, steps, flings into a body
flip through the air to land
as astonished as we,
hands as full of something he found
somewhere between the taking off and the landing
as the goldfish bowl of fishes and water
crouching which he lands on light feet and offers.

The fish jumped in the new bowl he held
as if they had just been birthed by sunlight.
Though we met no old-timers who recalled,
I've checked the encyclopedia.
It was a very famous goldfish bowl
even in a land where acrobats fly.

Sounds fishy? Open your eyes. You blind naysayers
are as raucous as the gibbons in the San Francisco Zoo,

our favorites. Jump in the swim of things.
Know your element. The laws he fooled over our eyes
were but the shadows of good things to come.
A great door was opened for us.
Out of empty hands into open eyes emerge
ombres chinoises like the white shadows of Glendower's Wales.

Big Daddy, it was a magic mountain
and you did it with silk.

If there's a dark elegy up this sleeve,
musing hasn't found it.
With a twinkling of an eye, concentration, and Carl Sandberg's spit
you made us see
but not everything.

CHINESE PAINTING

he says to a tree: my masters have been famous drunkards
     the emperor falls from his morning chair
     his women wait words to praise him
tapestries crown the mountains
     plunge exhausted animals
     held by the dead hands of fishermen
why must there be the other world
               than sleep?

DOGWOOD EASTER IN N.C.
for C. E. L.

Spring comes like popcorn here.
On the way to school the trees of Main Street
are nipped newborn
fisted in buds. Just so.

By lunch, homeward, ready for a rest,
they've opened like a freshman's face
or someone's older,
as fresh as an open hand
in whose palm you pick wild flowers.

With plentitude like this
for us a burnt grain at the bottom
will suffice.

IN MEMORIAM WM. B. HIGHT, JR.

Fine as frog's hair
he refined each tale
measured assayed
appreciated fool's gold.

In the beginning was the voice over
matter whose stones sprang golden warriors.
The apprentice magicked stumbling into competent
built toward the master class.
Perfection likes Hight.

Where does a voice arise? Out of what clay?
He taught not to fly by smoked mirrors.
This dross was magicked to sterner stuff
because if you drop your guard
in our profession as in the cloth's

the lie flies. The lie flies
fits unlike a moth not in the flame
but checkered on unclipped wings.
We pedagogues of sham and mirror
teach by smoke and error.

This man had a nose for the bogus
which came from love of the Logos.
No logos ever came of the bogus.
The world's gone lilliput.

A voice like every whorl is tuned.
At an old radio face we listen when the day's gone asleep.
It's dark aside, lights out on our street.
Ahush the ballroom dances in the big band sound.

But the strutters can't hear it nor the fretters.
The world's gone lilliput.
At trendy city where mendacity's at the ready
projectors build for a day.

The great bland countenances
as if for the world to worship and the mighty despair chump-dome.
If it's not worth doing it's not worth doing well.

In those days he descried the works of the mighty with-
out despair, made straight the way,
prepared a school, kept the traffic moving
with automatic shift he knew the way to the egress.
When launched his ships floated. His coliseums still fill.

Who holds the rain? In those days there were
no doubts. Under strict generosity the jocund land
prospered cornucopic.
Where the leaders rejoice with trembling the people prosper.
Our lot was full.

Caesar lifted the field
glasses to the arts of teachers, July experienced, learning loved.
For him the A-team was ready to cross the Alps.
He thought tall and like Hannibal preferred it
when a plan came together.

At the briefing our minds concentrated on the very
sharpened pencil and the code. The man was a planner.
In tie and jacket, starched and sweltering, the lieu-
tenants were at the ready for the General.
The birthday troops rejoiced with the trembling.

———

Respect's not an aspect in easy reach for all.

Life's a tall tale that vaunts a day of young
yet cheered and checked by the self-same sky
holds in perfection but a little moment.
Hight joined the Bard's stories and verse
and could expand or be terse.

The sky was his oyster.
He's in the midst of life in a single room.
A man breaks into laughter pulled down by contraptions.
Pulled down by contraptions breaks a man into laughter.
We gathered life by him and rejoice with trembling.

In Epypt he and the sphinx swapped riddles, maybe smoked camel's
dung. He could riddle a yarn. He could keep a secret
and the boy in him for surprises that carried
firecrackers and a snake in the pocket. When he uncovered the turkey
you never knew for sure what was flying.

Thunder is good, thunder is impressive—with Mark,
who no less than our pal fit not neat into metrical feet,
he opined it's lightning does the work.
He delivered the telling remark.
Like Sam and like Will, the Twain,
Bill enjoyed a laugh
with Falstaff
but ran the place
with the confidence of a Christian with four aces.

Some things won't bend to kindness.
Alien as a goat's the gotch eye stunts the squint kills
the straight facts
the fast and louche elide.

Bend geometry and call it Einstein.
The seats of the scornful fill quickly.
Who stands in the judgment?
The seats of the scornful are orchestra

and toads swell the music.
The house lights are hushed.
"The Sky Does Not Fall For A Lie"
is the show. It's Our Town.

His was a rich pasture under ample heavens.
The ungodly are not so.
Holy Moses goes the limit
but knows the limit.
Pastures run by the rivers of water

and rejoice with trembling. The wind blows
song goes on in other voices.
Fresh runners will carry the torch to the Promised Land.
He knew how to roll the stone away
and whose help he needed to do it.

NO FORWARDING ADDRESS
to J. S. W., poet-fisherman

I knew Isaac Walton in the sixties
and rising seventies
when he was casting every sentence
far out to the inevitable moment
the line turned to muse's tangled maenad hair

he pulled it in wet
with a colored fly left high over the stream
to be cut free like words from a dictionary
from flannel canvas and the felt hat of a fellow fisherman

flies bright in the palm
fast in the stream
each cast was always meant for the big one
though in our day the sixties and rising seventies
his soul knows what passes now for fishing
is fishy art arty

the white water's finished
there's only friendly fellows
that like their fish like their words
tame and on a platter

LAURA'S SLEEPER: A TONDO

It is a world to hang up round

which opens a space
blue and pink
Rolling along the wall
growing in its own color
Lifts and sinks light
stopped never yet in rest
complete but filling.

Try to know her season: winter sound
autumn gathered
summer sifting
springtime listing.

She is between the first and second vermouth.

Her breathing eases us, complete but filling.
What she has forgotten, we wish we could forget.

Yes.

Outside, a cyclist whistles.
Two floors up, a window opens.

THE MOON

Though the dark sickle of the gibbous moon is
  slender now,
soon a fan will open to form the circle umbrageous
  on an antique loom of Han.
The delicate shadow yearns for her coming roundness.
  Where do you see this in our sublunary world?

—Hsüeh T'ao

A RESTLESS MOURNER

SPRING OPENS

The ice releases its final suicides.
With open eyes they stand up asleep
stiff in old conviction like fathers.

In fields they blow upward the earth.
Last spring I thought about them too, two Jims from Texas, two friends,
in this woods road where mud and puddles still show winter tracks,

tired of game unworthy of them.
Wildlife again stalks the motorcycle ruts
and spore in the spring sun matches pinewood yellow.

Tall and stern, each tried to see how much breath he could suck
out of a gun barrel.
These trees stand blasted, enraged, against a new spring,

ice splinters in their stormy heads.
They remain at attention and still in range.
In the seasonal thaw suicides pocket the woods.

On a far green hill poofs from enemy batteries
blow away in gusts.
This is not the eighteenth century.

ICARUS OVER STANFORD UNION PATIO

at my table birds litter the trays
        hairy short black blasé
they stalk questions through food and glass

in the bookstore at my back
        the Han text mistranslates thus:
        —why did the boy bite the bird?
        because its cawing brought bad luck

such broken logics of life
        scratch my neck like a furious woman:
debating champs junketed for the weekend
        strut in sport shirt parrots
the immigrant's broom scrapes the terrace
        and the ponderosas lift in the wind
an opposing boy and girl grimace
        as he offers egg at fork-end
and all the while settling on the torn Campus Report
        cowbirds strut the print inquisitive
        chopped plumes quite proud

two students pass:
        —after cracking up your bike you what?
        spent ten days in Crete
        before a month in London sick bay

purple stocking and henna hair perches
        in the next table's trash
she writes the air with a smoking reed
she and her friend in canary cackle
        over myths and foul conception
in the shade of the California shedding tree

tonight she'll fly to her nest
which is a place of no rain
the music of water is pumped in by pipe
       until her eyes close at last
       and off the sheet
       into an obvious rug of purple
       her hand drops like a plover

from my table I arise
and bowlegged birds pitch off like sailors

SAM'S BACK

At the corner place Mr. J studies the sky to bring rain.
How close are concentration and magic,
magic, the precise mystery. Focus, do not think.
Betty calls on the phone, says get home or burn.
Life only promises. The spot on her cheek will always flame.
In the war, reports Samuel, we'd get knocked back twice,
call in the artillery—whole trees would disappear.
Could there be a breathing thing? In those little holes knocked out
VC'd awake and run out with blood streaking
out of their ears and nose to shoot us. Oh, they were dedicated.

Study it. Sparkling through grass and trees is the October sea
where it will fly like birds sailed from the hands of city urchins
who've just found the ocean. Mr. J remembers:
a grain of sand gave up into mud, grew a flower,
flexed into a knot, gourded, then rolled free as a baby.
He pulls apart the curtains and sees.

On the reclaimed channel Sam circles the dune buggy, which belches
            heads home.
Betty in the house burns paper figures in obscene positions.
The paper, lit, tugs, releases to become gray lettuce to her ravish-
ment.
A pit of soot settles spent. Burnt brows thank heavens sleep.
All my cabbage heads stack up in Genghis Khan's captured kitchens.
She looks up. Her two magicians come through the door.

The stables are ready for their neigh, the motorways for their passage.
You move to the window. The darkened garden of your life
is there, the streams, trees, lawns, the impish pit

where you fell. You never meant it, never,
only to build with care a few pleasures and contests and triumphs.
By the sycamore there an imp in the machine

spilled your wit. The muddy spot must puzzle you.
It's only a simple yard
where a man might break his neck

by his own hand.
No need to wander there then or now, my friend.
It is one deed you cannot do twice.

Now you, the younger man at the bench, work your father's work.
The reader and I are watching too,
rising behind you, falling back, failing, returning again and again

like dust or Scots mist this Christmas Eve morning.
More than one phantom mountains over you
as you study his plans and draw with his pencil in his light.

DEATH OF AN AUTOMOBILE EXECUTIVE
BY HIS OWN HAND

I too would visit my son at my workbench
amid my hoarded tools, under the lights I wired,
my boy caught in dreams over father's blueprints.

I too would take my place where you loom
over the son working to complete the father's drawings.
I too would study his hand swing over the plans.

It is a visitation richly comprehended,
though above his head you are only mute and invisible.
He cannot see or hear you. How he must wonder!

What turned on him?
Did he trust the wrong truth?
We, masked, would have walked the Himalayas together,

traveled through valleys and over the rivers of Nepal
up past monasteries into the snow country.
We would have planted our flag.

Maps of the world gleam on the wall over the table.
Beyond, in the unlit garage, lurk unborn Bentleys.
Classic Fords to be assembled ghost the hanger.

FAILING EXAMS

Hard for the moon to keep its glory at sunrise,
Hard for a broken man to take heart.
Who says the whole world blooms in spring?
Alone I watch the frost on the petals.
The strong hawk, its powers gone, sickens.
The wren wheels high on borrowed wings.
Put down, put down again.
I feel as though they'd cut me open with a sharp knife.

—Meng Chiao

PROFOUND GONDOLA, OR THE BAND WAS PLAYING AS THE TITANIC WENT DOWN, APRIL 14, 1912: A POLITICAL ALLEGORY FOR '92, WITH ECHOES OF A VISIT TO HARRY'S BAR OPPOSITE THE OLD PARIS OPERA HOUSE WITH GILL

Maestro Marconi sounds the deeps. The time grows fainter, faint.
Sounds never die, Jacques. Are you really dead? O my poor drowned doll.
The persistence of childhood plays on.

On the deck the band pauses at a tilt to sing.
Leviathan awash surfaces on cue, the sword-swallower slips
the long ship down his throat, HRRAH go the icebergs.

If a music box found on the bottom by bending marauders
would it entertain? No sound dies, the Maestro says, jamais Jacques.
Fainter only grows in circles. It grows around

continental drifts. It grows in the Philippine Sea
around the pings of torpedoes warships. Which corridor?
Which labyrinth? Where does your wealth lie?

The music box plays dogfish moseys over the dance floor.
A dull bottom creature bobs with a bubble.
In Père-Lachaise Chopin persists to the moving of giant pianos.

Thin ladies and gentlemen elegantly shredded wait.
High heels takes the salted almond. Guy shakes the bruised highball.
Where's Jacques? Every skull turns when she slowly floats in.

Is Jacques dead now? Your skin is beautiful, but it tears so.
Your smooth soul prowls, but nearer my God to Thee.
Profound gondolas await us. Lean this way. He sits somewhere
        in royal ease.

FAULKNER IN CHARLOTTESVILLE

Faulkner held his brother's face
together on the way home from the plane crash
the only time a side sagged
he took a hand off for the bottle
for fifty miles he laid out the body for dressers
the remains nailed in pine
under dirt and a stone
when he later saw that face times again
it too looked drunk

he stored it all away
while the engine ran the journey lap after lap
until he saw it
in the punch bowl at the Farmington Hunt Breakfast
where he and an elderly lady in veils drank
all three gallons in the batch

he saw those live eyes in the whiskey face
(it was bright autumn in the call of dogs)
rising and falling with oranges and lemons
by a lump of ice heavier than a head

he drank while there was time

IN THE DEVELOPING TRAY WITH EVA BRAUN

In an upstairs apartment in the Old Dominion
the veteran offered three trophies of the spoils
that flew out of the Führer's nodus in high Berchtesgaden.

The first bit of allied booty we held
with Vernon and Betsy and company was Mein Kampf,
whose personal heft my hands the tight skin have since felt.

We know now the masterwork he did not script himself
with pen but breathed over amanuenses who brought it
to sheet, signature, and boards, and gave wings to its gravity.

An evening just out of the fifties that war
and his breathing were now well over, and Eva Braun's.
We were just a young married couple. The time comes in and out of focus.

Souvenir number two, also heavy, was Göring's private railway
tablecloth with Hakenkreuz picked out of linen center and corners.
Such fingerwork takes the hours away.

The gift of eyes may sometimes win a pension.
Many a New World dinner of turkey was savored
over this still stiff handwork. Eva, herself

the third spoil, as shimmery as the silver frame
about her face and figure, surely stood as nature
plumped her womanhood in a vineyard of Third Reich nudes.

Her beloved, initially a painter, would have higher justice
done to hank and hide, had ambition's eye
stiffened in oils. The tooth of the receiving cut canvas

———

no artist forgets, the paint in the mouth,
the fingers in the brush.
Forget that, whatever the talent,

it went elsewhere into strangeness
and led us all by the nose. The world could not have been
a place more evil—but let history in the subjunctive lie.

We only have the photograph in black and white. Or
should have. For Betsy, waiting for her husband
to return from foreign wars, unwrapped the trophies

sent ahead, gasped perchance, and in good humor
called over her friends for judgment and highballs.
The gentlemen might have toasted the lass

and grown sympathetic before that bottom power.
The picture of the lass under all those eyes
didn't stand a chance. No disporting with the fiend here.

The rump, in short, the hair, the charm was tossed with the trash
sales and boches. The combed hair of the children of the house
replaced the handmaiden's in the silver frame, their gaze for hers.

Their posture we know because there they are,
now grown, prospering, bearing their own.
What was hers? Torque? Did her eye connect with ours

with a tilt of the glass? For recent diggers say at last
her eye quickened not only to her leader's. She must have tired
of the imagination of his heart before the final days.

So fit as a fresh statue of liberty she
arrived in the raw to be reborn on the shore of raw starts
and then was put away for the children in Lynchburg,

where Tom and I committed Wer reitet so spät to memory
and daughters of the Erlkönig stole us away.
The barren mother of Adolf's brood, Eve's avatar was

bare as innocence tossed away. Mein Kampf rests
on the shelf. The tablecloth may to this day drape
under dinner on Ben Franklin's national bird.

The essence of Eva had blown off in the breeze.
It all seems feathers.
The photographer in Berlin who washed her about

may have dropped a tear in the developing tray.
Could a lover's second glossy darken against his ribs
in the family crematorium while the crime was blazing?

The rest is left to us. We sift through embers
and squint through the private eye of the long dead.
It's not easy to miss mother Eve's glimmer in the crooked garden.

A RESTLESS MOURNER COMES CALLING
TO A CEMETERY IN CHARLESTON

The sundial says noon but it's three: only a summertime story.
The mourner's pushed the gate open and passed from the street to the
churchyard of graves.
Who strolls, touches monuments. What remains?
The processioners have stopped in their places.

Here disease took a daughter. Here one youth was enough for a son.
Here the stone dove of the wife flies off to eternity.
Grandfather's ship sets sail. The marble says
a soldier came back to lie down in this bed.

Inside the church someone weeps where it is sacred and cool.
The guest strolls, drifts. By the back wall a pause. Hush!
Under the dark trees a newer body's form has pressed the grass,
and he's left the black clothes, a fold of newspaper,
                lost and found, sailings.

He must have rested his head on this infant's stone.
The grass is soft underfoot. Stands still in his lair.
Anyone here? Hello? Poised, an arm outstretched
over which to drop a pall. An arm is frozen. Hello?

It's afternoon; the squirrels rattle in the hot live oaks.
But there's only the sooty clothes he left.
Under a rotten palm shirt and trousers are laid out like pajamas.
Pat Mullarky reads the neck.

Kick a bottle. Many have sailed into this place to beach.
Fleets of glass ships lie in the earth
the depth of a drunkard's hand.
All messages have been removed.

Pat hiding stripped and watching his bed? A vigil?
It's still. Only stamped glass. Over the wall a truck dies.
Mullarky the philosopher pushes a frond aside to watch.
The guest looks behind the tree and then up into the branches.

A cat from nowhere jumps to the wall, arches a black back,
         curls a spiritual tail,
disappears. Pat? A brick flies. In the street an engine starts
for the getaway. Escaping in the prison truck?
The mourner waits over his rags. There is readiness, but no.

The face of the sundial blurs. Must go,
must retreat before the mortmain of this plot of a seaside city
in which shallow graves the quarts and pints and splits,
muldoons of carry-me-away, sink deeper.

No cat on the wall, not even a sob through the church windows.
In his moon-crossed currents, if he had spoken, Pat might have told
how the dead swim in the ocean.
To leave, the gate is no heavier to lift, no lighter.

AN INSCRIPTION IN STONE
in the Rear Court of Meditation at Broken Hill Monastery

On a clear morning enter an old temple
just as the sun strikes the top branches.
Push along a turning path
through dark places where
grasses and trees rise
by the buried shrine.
Mountain light gladdens the whistling birds.
A shadow in the pool
empties your heart.
All the mountain sounds are shut out.
Musical stone and bell toll alone.

—Ch'ang Chien

TREMBLING UNDER THE THUNDER

East wind sigh,
sift an easy rain over the hibiscus pond
trembling under the thunder.

A gold toad has locked his secret mouth over the latch.
Where the incense burns, enter there.

A jade tiger is hauling the silk rope.
Water lifts from the well time after time.

Once Lady Chia hid behind a screen to spy on
  her young man.
Once the Princess of Lo River left her pillow
for the accomplished Prince Wei.

Your spring heart.
may it never burst with flowers.
An inch of burning is an inch of ash.

—Li Shang-yin

SINGING GIRLS IN THE BRONZE BIRD TOWER

A lady fills a bowl of wine.
Behind her reaches back an autumn scene a thousand
  miles deep.
Stone horses have stretched out in the dewy smoke.
What is the language of sadness?
A wind rising in the trees on the grave murmurs the
  sound of the singing.
The full gowns are crushed in the lookout tower.
Stinging eyes stare at the sacrifice of flowers
  on the table.

—Li Ho

VENUS HOLDS BY THE LIP OF THE NEW MOON

Legend lies that geese of great weight
walked off the river beds and
with their creaking wings adrag
scooped out shallow valleys and bays
from Boston to Concord.
Hysteric students by the Charles
still hear their stony honk in spring,
and in the Square with each new subterranean bar
a print of web in rock is found
along with cannon balls and the infrequent femur.

In the Ha' Penny is a corner with a seat as soft as down
where history came back strong last night:
'twas the Geneva Craze (drunk a-penny,
dead-drunk tuppence) which struck
deep into their liquid selves
while the talk moved au courant
and as controlled as T'ang rooflines
against razorback mountains of sugarcane and slate and jade peaks
where students in T-shirts freeze six a season.
Of the ribs of that ancient style the saw was misquoted,
"Thousand year beauty loosens very slowly."
Even the olive in the deepest martini in town
goes by trireme back to groves sacred to Athena
below Delphi and not many miles from the place where three roads meet.

Here, when the wind is up
and Venus holds by the lip of the new moon,
Emerson's wife is still seen to stand like a torch
and Hawthorne silhouettes a stopped window dreaming
beauties of the many-venomed earth.

The Old Manse is cold and boarded to the chance embracing couple,
snow off the boughs whipping past the shutter
as lovers click tiny pictures in a scene.
Except the occasional smell of powder and sound of musketry
near the statue of the Minute Man,
that's all that's left
under the goose-down sky.

BUFFALO WATCH OUR EYES

GUESSING THE ALLIGATORS
AT THE CHARLES TOWNE LANDING

Guess the alligators.
In the gardens where couples marry
folks lean over the bridge: they love the mud so!
Oh they're waking up to slide our way!
Ancien régime.

Best they love your thinking it. Watch the patriarch.
Lidded, dripping, he awaits the statistical drop.
He plays the odds like an ancient boulevardier
with a gleam in his monocle:
Eighty years sez I win.

The rail creaks lunch around the noon of this century.
What's the race? Call again
in some millennium.
Memory is dynastic.
The short decades are for grandnephews and grandnieces
who need patience.

I'll rest and tell myself
jokes in mud. Old ones, yes, but they are very good.
Ageds appreciate like veterans.
I recall your grandfather's boot. His leg.
Second honeymoon, an old romantic, sensible brides must agree.
His cane is here somewhere still.

Conquests ago I caught a bird of a bride
by her starched middle, though her young gentleman leaned
and reached with a riding crop.
But she loved my wisdom,
wait and grow wise. Only his hand I snagged,
yet from the sound he gave his true voice too.

Mon vieux, many
have posed on my bridge in pictures.
Senators and street cleaners, grooms and bridesmaids,
wise virgins and foolish—I'll want a bite of all yet.
This bridge of ropes lasts long
but breaks as sure. The truth will win,
even if it takes two lifetimes.

Watch him from up here. His crust is old.
We guess high, he guesses low.
There's only one guess in the mud
but long experience.

ODE TO THE NEW SPORTS COMPLEX PARKING LOT
DURING A BIG SNOW IN RED CLAY COUNTRY
ON THE SEMICENTENNIAL OF THE RAPE OF
NANKING AFTER THE VISIT OF THE BLUE CRANE

This might be a cup washed in raspberry juice
or a rock thrown through the window dressing,
a cup of hands or a rifle butt into the blind face.
History is being written, rewritten, history books for war,
the Chinese expansion, from East to West, Japan to the US of A.
Educators everywhere gently burying your history,
"renewing official records, bringing the past up-to-date."

More snow covered the rabbit tracks crossed Thursday morning
after Odin's storm blew through the Black Watch.
The forest paths were chaste through the glistening trees.
Saturday, tramping, tracking snow imps, we puffed and wheezed
beyond Erwin Lodge, stopped a sudden moment:
until the cheep cheep, bits of leaf skipping in the trees,
bits of dark feather flitting across the snow, wet brown white,
twittering, silencing, astounded
us booted in snow dotted with twig feather leaf.
We were surrounded by the invasion of the junkos,
the infiltration of the chickadees, the LBJs.
A shadow stirred. Homeward we passed the stone lodge
standing for two dead brothers in uniform.

Wednesday this morning in the open, craters, angry red hillocks
had broken through the excellent feather bed of sugar.
Better skirt the parking lot of the future, break a leg
where one day fans will park their roadsters thousandfold.
If the moon is cheese, red clay and creamed cheese is
        our pooked moonscape.

_____

Fresh digging tree, this very morn: jawbone of the machine.
Mum's the word! The bulldozers are invited back
to celebrate the rape of Nanking, 1937, a semicentennial event
for your calendar.

Get your history right: the elderly lady and her daughters and
granddaughters now receive the soldiery in the street, at home,
in her hospital bed with her eyes quite open.

Far in the distance from a sky box
a vision shimmers. Pit bulldozers
guided by phantom children
like toy earth-movers
growl, doze, crawl over the moonscape looking for stumps.

Isn't there a pit bulldozer lease law in our village?
Wild dogs pull down a child in Amherst, Virginia, and kiss his face.
I see men as trees, walking. I see men as trees, walking.
Walking by, a morning before the neighbor's pond froze,
a water bird lifted off the water. The shadow might have covered the pond,
the great wings creaking at lift-off, folded dropping on the shore,
mighty, as if it had impregned the original abyss.
The neighbor not young in hearing replied, "The blue crane?"
Migrating? A visitor? Flying through? "It lives here all-year-around."
I squinted. Its visit had captured us without hearing aid and blear-eyed.
Invisible, inaudible, it has not yet returned.
We see men as trees, walking. We hear trees as men, talking.

CHRISTMAS LINES: THE VILLAGE STAGE

Bushes grow on his pate while he sits in his Christmas tent.
"How old is this troll?" Cries for Darvon, this ruminant December,
the tenth and deadliest month. When a troll explodes
bits of his hide confetti the valley all the way
to Lillehammer. The villagers laugh to a man.
The fire in this belly needs stoking.

Up and down the season's streets we drive
heavy limos. Surely things will happen in newspapers.
Wires light the hair and neck of the Cedar of Village Green.
Now a carol palms by the brick church wall
and over our leprous sward. A week till Eve.
Revelers ride a VW down Manhattan with one wheel off,
sparks from sleigh laugh, circus car of sparks.
Now in their shacks the poor are burning, burning.

In Florida the widow freezes with her icy mite. The orphan sinks.
To the north, lightening the sled,
brides are fed to the wolf on Bothnia's racing gulf.
Ahead the traffic light changes. The popcorn is ready,
glowing in its dome. It drops, we lurch.
The room on floor four is smoking at the window.
Now watch for the blazing bed. Note the mattress of sulphurous flame.
At this point they come out for the fall, the long gainer, the gainer
        and a half.
Here, if you are still, above them at the smoky balustrade,
unlisted guests spread their wings to fly like angels.

THE EMPIRE STRIKES BACK

Nine-year-olds are playing in Chambers Building's long halls
when it's cool in the summer slowdown.
On the top floor it's dark except for exit lights
and what pirates smuggle in through cracks.

Joel lingers by the stairwell, hunkers.
He picks a shard of light off the floor
thrown from a high, forgotten fanlight
and lets it play like colored glass.

Sabers and wolves' heads and swans he shapes in his yellow hand.
In this old building with its bald head
the only sun slides in under the patch over its dim eye
or where a tooth is out.

Sounds below. The enemy is coming!
They are moving up the elevators
and up the stairs.
They seek your gang.

The boy sets the shard and (jump!) dodges.
The corridor is a clean sweep of shadows.
Whispers hide like pirates' dingoes beyond the fire.
Joel and comrades (into north and south

the legions of the Empire have debouched and advanced deadly)
are cut loose in their dark, safe vessel. On the floor glows
the low dish of Joel's filled
and set back where the boots come marching.

DESERTION AND RECONSTRUCTION

Monique took the baby and moved out fast
leaving the sun in the floor wasting table and chairs
two last-chance avocados on the sill
a map on the wall of a dusty country
      shape as strange as a parrot's shadow
and a panther face in the tile floor
      sleeping with his eyes open.

Her lovechild of wine and time fostered
in a blowing curtain embrace
   the wall white-red through the gown of her
      mother's body
had laughed and cried at the doorstep
   now untrod—gone now
and from the passing left
              no privacy in the empty mind.

How much time? Now the house of comedians
    panthers face in tile
    under melons edging the bright square
is set for a millennial dig.
In stringed archaeological squares (what might be
   evidence?)
      lift one French loaf from white ash
      shake out the chairs
      weight the stone fruit
and take down the ash map marvel from the buried wall.

SUBMARINE OFF OUR UNBELIEVING COAST:
WRIGHTSVILLE BEACH, 1991

The coastal warrior by the dock waits in dozy waves
for the run down the whaleroad
where we lift and fall in summer's swell.
If they do live, the gods of law live in the heartland.

Though at war, this is first about a happy memory.
Something points to the victory decals on a coastguard cutter
off Wrightsville Beach last summer: a flower for a weed,
a snowflake per snowboat?

What burst of rapture awaits the persimmon?
I understand the grip of God and sea. There is a victory to be won.
Poke out a pirate's eye and send his sweetbreads below
for the shark's nose. The Old Testament is our right hand.

We let the rules slide. Honor's list drops at Rachel's strangled face
the drawing pencil. The rules are samely overall.

In Istanbul the Sephardic healer Madame Sara twists
a sympathetic table under a palm
unimpugned at 400 pounds.
Her charming fingers, my darling,

to heal the forces of gravity defy May
and June. I am no magician. I tell the military
I am a medium around whose restraint spirits close only.
After summer goes autumn leans into the wind.

They come into us now. In monthly gales
their manes ribbon in whinnies. Measure your breathing.

Somewhere a great mare waits to break.
While I see it twirls on a corner without a core.

Their spirit shoulders bare a sliding message.
The chest is tight below the throne.
Buffalo watch our eyes for a signal.
Where once we leaned on who oppress now,

they gather our rituals. They fill dishes
under white sheets in a bowl of purged blood.
Innocent once, to make visible these invisible messengers
I healed the first without camouflage of raiment.

Now rugs and gold has healing lured
as witness in her behalf.
Believers coax, importune
about the cuddly door.

Outsider, you who are looking in, try to remember:
the picture last week in a video in the Carolina Inn
flickers from the warrior resting by a Wrightsville dock
in the summer of 1991

to an earlier picture of happy John Dryden in
Houston, 1966. Sweet concinnity makes us all believers.
No turncoat poet, this submariner told tests below the sea surface
we shipped with Captain Nemo our dinner table over, a migraine
        sweating torpedoes.

Asleep after a day of drills fast
the day of the calendar so known to routine
tired when you turn over in the deckered bunk
the body may slip out in midair flip

———

back waffling in pad over under springs
at the nose. Discipline turns o'er sleep and dreams
without briefly the midshipman conscious.
Forty fathoms lullaby below.

Our atmosphere underwater sucks through the teeth.
Consider the cigarette. It toils not
neither does it spin. A light grows cold
between our comrade's fingers less Homeric.

Air is rationed, for just an unheroic spark burns on the tip.
We crew deliberate the smokes and make sensible book.
How much wind fills Mae West?
What of life is left we wonder when the kissing stops?

Depth charges drop by helloing echo.
We concentrate on the naming of the parts, the kissing of the firing pins.
We are short in stature, long in deed and boast.
Simple mediums to air fathoms over us, we are not magicians.

Somewhere in the squat of all of this is exhaling.
Spirit bodies like the rest of us need room to breathe in and out.
Today, somewhere in the falling November 1991
back in the present, AP reports a sighting:

a metal shark off the Portsmouth whaleroad that's been waiting since 1943.
You down there! Aren't you in a place where the law to kill
reaches all moving parts? Earn a persimmon on her conning tower?

THE TAO COMES TO DAVIDSON

SPOOKING A DEAD MAN'S COWS

Mr. McClamrock's been dead for six months
and in town they didn't even know.
Down the road at his house

his workshop (built his last year
in cinderblock all aroar like hades
at seven in the morning) is cold

these December mornings.
Yelling Goddamns at his grandchildren
(all sons) is now silenced.

A prophet save in his own country—
well, everybody round here
was scared shitless of him.

His farm pond steams by itself now,
barbwired in. I do remember a few cows though
one August day got up enough nerve

to put their forelegs in—
the chin of a cow on summer waters
—where's Constable? Not here.

I never saw a human near the place,
except for McClamrock and his grandsons,
and the last time I saw him up close

he gave me a lift in his truck
going to his new job as guard
at the McWhorter Nuclear Plant.

———

Pistol pushed down in the upholstery,
he had only time to say where he was headed
before he dropped me off.

Townsfolk for years said he'd lived
(supported a wife and house, truck, sheds, cows)
on insurance from an ancient piece of bad luck.

I thought about that this morning
when I walked by and spooked his cows.

TOWN DAY REMOVALS AND RENEWALS

The shoemakers here are all divines,
holy solely but whole soul too.

Mr. McKissick, who'd sew a boot and say 15 cents,
now has a pulpit in Charlotte,

city of churches once called.
Fred, still sloughed in original Liverpool,

now wrinkled Cornelius,
was bound low over heaps of pumps

when you left sole and heel last week.
Now translated like saint's relics for Town Day May,

Saturn's day on Main Street by the Caboose, a new throne room,
his face shines beatitude over new counter and sign

though the removal's been as alone as death and no grandson
providence-provided for the lathe

who'd flown to the air force had gone.
So Moreland taunted your boots were lost

and you bootless and landlost,
abandoned in the old shop for bulldozing

the gone double derelict, an outrigger sized 13½ AA each.
But collect them now whole again on Town Day.

The Lord provideth, says Fred.
Beatitude blazes forth translated from Liverpool

———

to a fresh sign and name on the fresh street
of the Sandal Maker.

Customer-found he will be.
You walk out in reborn shoes

swapped in his shop the old one on your feet
for the new from his hands,

your name in your hand taped now inside the heel
of a set of broken crepe soles

to be twisted and tacked to the new.
The true trades never age.

The dictionary takes latchet to las, noose, snare;
see lace, which says see lacere, allure;

see delight, allure away.
John the Baptist put his hand to new latchets,

new life to new tongues.
Beyond delight no IE line stretches out beyond.

No bird catcher slogged through ur-bogs of shift,
umlaut ablaut um ab um um laut laut laut.

Somewhere in the middle distance she was lost
and she arose again in the middle distance

like the Madonna inside the Door, the lady lovely
who would not step into the rain with her babe

only last week when you heart-looked held the door, latched,
a look which has hung your guts high in the wind

and will return spring March thaw.
So you negotiated Mrs. Gamp outside in the wet

while inside wrung the sheets of an overseaed three-master.
Sitting Samson waits for blindness.

Posed, snap. Out of the negative dished
floats a positive head, hair in the dish, lacing.

Oil locks the king!
Stop, my child, forget not the dust of the hand, the clay fingers.

In your spit the dust twists.
Make, see. See, make.

A spider close to earth is tying dew-drifted lace.
Thong has a taproot beneath the tree,

twengh, to press in on, twinge.
Await the tapping on the boards of the risen Town Day twinge,
snick, quick, sthnap.

It's outside, Fred's new shop,
the lassies are dancing, the Blue Grass Spring.

The boards tap.
Thinking what do I walk in I forgot above, I'll report
like a sixshooter:

———

yours is the knitting, the knitting ours
by weight ninety pounds, and as quick as tricks.

WALKING THROUGH DISTRICT PRISON, TAICHUNG, TAIWAN

       in the skills room among prison machines
       rough and smooth
                        edge and empty
       triangles cylinders
                        hooks and cups
       dim inmates are fabricking wares

outside in sun we linger the compound garden
           where unnamables pruned in bush
           set out Shang birds and shrubbery deer
           a horse waiting under her leafy saddle
           twin seabeasts with sticks for horns
                                thorns for udders

: clipped creatures in local bush
who circle a low pagoda trimmed in broken glass

towards us in the sparkling garden
men in asbestos relax over guests
(their mouths filled with silver smiles)
and lean out the dark shuttle room

next door a squint:
       in a stone room
       scraped with knives
       separately sit three on heels
       (one rubs his metal teeth)
       and watch the dwarf peach growing outside their
        window
: hunkering recidivists

                ———

all are inmates who dream of mountain paddies
  footponds of blackfish
  carved boars on Lion's Head Mountain
dream among half-sunken boats
  cloud mountains fruit in the market
  fishermen on riverlost boats

what is round
                asks caresses
what unclean
             scraping
to these dim prisoners fabricking over smooth machines

CONVERSATION WITH A MUSIC BOX
IN A RED CLAY ROADHOUSE

Madame Wurlitzer
in the corner,
how do you keep
up your weight! Sorry fate!
So heavy in your widow's weeds?
Dark and dull and out of the way,
are you blind or just asleep?

It's a long way
from the Ponce de Leon,
whose sign in neon
seemed to say,
"Just start the music and watch me dance!"
Once flocked by the randiest
flâneurs that ever cried Temptation
you'd purr, "Life's for fun,"
and break an aria from the past
while dollars stuffed the piano glass.
Oh, they loved you, those permanent and paying guests,
in earlier days when hummed along by battered hedonists.

Now you're a red clay wallflower,
overdressed for this early hour
and waiting for a quarter's worth
of attention to open your public mouth
and cry. Great pleasure boat, as baubled
as a lapsed dancer's belly,
for a coin you'll mother a moan
for any son of a number
in blue grass, rock or scheherazade.

Your loves are past. Here they strictly clog
and local farmers are the only charmers.

Boy, I've got silver in my elbows
and silver in my toes.
My jaw's full of nickels
and my teeth are full of holes.
I've got quarters in my gut
and lyrics full of smut.
My chins jingle with the dimes—
I ain't sad, I'm fine!

You won't get a penny back
for all the songs I've sung,
and that's my rule, Jack.
I haven't flung my last fling yet.

So come aboard and play
(today won't last forever

and it won't come back never)—
just poke any number.
This may be the Broken Anchor
and a long way from town,
but it ain't church neither—
there's still fun around!

AFTER PASSING THE EXAM

The dreck of former days is not worth bragging about.
Today I have let my mind go wild, and
the spring breeze has made my wishes come true as
      fast as my horses' hooves can gallop.
In one single day I have plucked myself to death
      among all the flowers of the nation's capital.

—Meng Chiao

DRESSING UP TO BLOW A TUNE TO THE MOON

You see, athletes need the shirt size,
said she, but when a little guy

comes in here with an 18½ neck he's
got to be a horn player. His eyes squeeze.

His cheeks can pump up an automobile flat
with trumpet tunes of divine lift.

Was the Sunday spare we changed
pumped with trumpet lungs? Inspiration and extra cash?

A song went along in a wheel up Grey Road to town.

He just bought a cummerbund at Mitchell's in Belk SouthPark.
You know, said she, evening dress has returned to waltz.

For the gentleman attire is an easy tuxedo avec corsage,
but the lady shifts belle among expensive dresses restless.

Wherein may she dwell among them all?
The necks of the ladies and the collars

of the gentlemen sniff starch and the perfume *Ancien
Régime*. A flirtation of scent

gooses from the far side of the Revolution
when noble heads bobbed before the bonjour of the executioner.

Your glamour, was it only lost? The knitters click cluck.

But at this moment a particular party in Manhattan dances dinner. Out the
window we admire

the Empire State Building lit. The city is an oyster
whose gleam makes a pearl. As the toasts

go round, we lift faces and glasses up
toward the dock on top

once envisioned to moor the floating airships of the empire.
Our gaze catches the first spaceship atop fire

hurrahing off toward the moon.

Later that champagne night with bubbles popping
in a cloudy club on the street below

we push to the front to see a trumpet loosen his colar
and play headache brass.

I can hardly breathe.

Bring the picture home. You are night steering
south down Interstate 77. You need to change a tire.

Air keeps the world afloat.
That Manhattan morning we watched the brass notes

fly away and collect at the mooring up
there on the tall building. Lend us your eyes. Can't you

see the zeppelins calling in and out of song trumpet
as they top off the NationsBank snowpeak?

We're dressing up to blow a tune to the moon.

DUCK SOUP ON A WINTER MORN

Most of the pond ducks on Griffith Street have gathered in
the last tongue of water rippled through the windshield
that froze boiling water (holy Pyrex!) when we left this morning.
Electric cows were in the morning field,
and Nabob glowed like Napoleon's charger.

Now we on 77 race a school bus on parallel 21
(its windows are black as silver) and junior highers
against the administration wall at Alexander
hunch sun in the smoky minutes before the bell.

Back, the few fowl not in the last free winter float
duck walk their domain of ice like workmen at McGuire Nuclear Power
going through the gate. A boy at the back with their lunch pails trails.

It's all business-like divinity on this steaming winter morn;
all know their ice, as well as their swim and bob.

REACHED BY LIGHT AMONG
THE EMPTY SCHOOLROOMS

The day snows alone, no mops
in the halls, not a boss,
not a customer for our product, snow
through the door and window
left open rises
reprises after Egyptian reprises
alone in the places of the sand Ozymandian.
It hangs on that three-story cedar
and certainly on the roof overhead.
Outside sportswomen throw snowballs, footballs, soccer balls,
balls smashed with hockey sticks, jai alai pops pelota,
a tennis racket dices ice for snow salad.
Over the green sward of the billiard table taps the misty cue ball.
Let's dance a waltz
with the mop. Spoon.
Historians will chart the arc of our frozen breath.
There's a distant juggler tosses atop Mt. Everest.

"Nope! We lumber belumped. The halls of rooms are lined with
          wool and gloom,"
they say. But we say nay to their say, they and their sullen friends.
There is no war. None goes on now.
In the world is green Joseph
leads a child to England's mountain green,
her green & pleasant land.
Hold it up: as the blessing falls
all are touched to dance.

MISSED THE BARD AT MLA THIS YEAR

It was only a handful of colleagues who said he was coming.
But they were always the dependable ones.
His name on the program?
As a discussant. Oh my prophetic soul!
But it was no good finding him in the 666 sections
(my copy was defective and still got left
at a publishers-drunk).
Maybe the registration lines.
No, he could have managed that, patience and
          an eye on the luggage.
Maybe the snow got him down
though the only glimpse I got of
anyone looking a thing like him was standing in the
          middle of the street
at one-thirty a.m. with his face up to the flakes.
By then he would have been in his room writing
a new carnival of fools
Doll Tearsheet at his elbow pouring him another.
Gawd, Doll, listen to this line!
Probably still recovering two days after
getting on the plane at La Guardia
kicking himself for forgetting his hat
cold pated in New York City snow
like Bottom or Lear.

THE TAO COMES TO DAVIDSON IN ICE
TO FELL THE PATRIARCH

The first tiny wonderers who came before
Leviathan Stranded
were followed by detectives looking for the criminal,
investigative, counting rings,
estimating time and circumstances
(the only witness of the instant said
to be one nocturnal cameraman
caught by surprise and still underneath).
So proud, so stern, and so beached,
the last oak of a commencement address
(but so long to die!
last year's tree of May rotted
by September they say),
his limbs were too strong to give until
the chill could never be shaken off or out
of the sleeves of his overcoat—
an old man growing heavier and heavier until he fell.
"How could a granddaddy oak live so long
in such shallow soil?" they say
as they see the uncovered head of roots and clay.

Earlier, out Grey Road, backed by a wonderland of winter meadow
the first charm puckers
the face of a cow whorled through the fence
and chews a loop of frosty lettuce—
a riddle in bovine phiz between rails and arched
with a boa of silver cedar
(somebody's taste in beauty and grub).

In the woods the bombardment has been lifted.
Some casualties stand still erect, headless, armless,

———

yellow splintered spikes, broken glass at their feet
(trek of the mastodon)
by a path crossed by suppliants
who bow bridge after bridge to climb or duck.
Above the hillside as high as the power line
peers the second creature, the head of the Blue Ox,

her muzzle drips with briny sludge.
Blue Babe on a bender!
But it won't last forever. With the thaw
we'll see which pines melt straight
of the ones that haven't pulled themselves out by the ankles.
Then all will return to water and mud.

At the top of the hill from the gate to the cross-country path
mid-soccer-field
a boy leaps and pauses
carrying a girl piggyback through the brittle.

Soon they walk and reach the road round the school
to the post office, the front campus.
They could have been leaping from boulder to boulder in the Ice Age.

A last look at the woods:
if some strength could spring the drawn trunks
now while all is sheeted fast,
they would fill the air with spangles
and the forest floor with swan heads and shard of chandelier.
Tiffany's after the Beast!
Or if the freeze never broke,
the glass blower's clipper could sail forever in her arctic rigging,
never float free,
and the saws of the workmen still be cutting ice.

TAKING OFF

OLD DAYS IN LEXINGTON
from the fifties

Lifting the razor, while the lecturer
bent his head over the royal woe of Lear,

into the space between two lines Bob began
to build a new ship for the fleet he ran

from a back row in class. Pocket gives a blade
kept at the ready he sets to shaving

prick point to the lead. Then he touches it
to that space between two ruled lines with such

intent a world within does grow. We
lean to watch his craft. We're lieutenancy.

A steel PT boat rears complete in hulk
inside two docks of shipyard. The work

is not done in some vast hangar controlled
by Navy but in a very narrow ruled

notebook far back in English class.
Etched hull, deck, torpedoes, flags are fore, aft.

At last on deck he tips in the full crew,
One by one, side by side, proud, in full view

upon an easy sea. Vision is armed!
The craft's been rigged by Bob with charms.

In and out of the frightened fire of search
lights we snake toward the marked ship's roll and lurch

———

in high seas and send the metal fish flying
that leaves the quick floating by the dead crying

out in flames. The oil catches. The ship bursts.
Red rays meet in a rising sun where first

the tin fish bunted the gaudy vessel
just under the water line. This lesson

the captain from Kyoto will not learn
again. Heavy field glasses with a firm

squint he lifts to scan for torpedo—
is he humming a tune from The Mikado?

And sees only as it scoots in motored
by PT pride and a little propeller

and strikes. The imperial battleship shudders,
rears, sliders under, imperial flags aflutter.

* * *

Shoemakers Holiday, Ralph Roister Doister,
Pamela, Shamela, get thee to a cloister.

Impotent, insistent, the heated teacher
is wasting his time on us and a feature

on his syllabus. It is a paradise
lost on us. With armed vision Bob splices

Daedalus' wings. Fugitives from science,
we made our way up the hill to the lines

of columns ruled by George Washington,
erect in wood, chalky in the sun

of Rockbridge County. From Liberty Hall
if you climb up to the ruins in fall

the sight of George amidst the purple, red,
rust, orange—seeing its gleam, fancy stops dead.

Why go further?—It flits to General Lee,
recumbent marble. Boys lost in the Maury

are called back all along the Chapel wall.
"Death loves a shining mark." We cannot recall

Tom or Jacques or Bill from his rendezvous.

*   *   *

PLEDGE PALS

We'd play a trick on Vernon, game him good.
Wally and I told Vernon (just to hood-

wink a fellow pledge) that Wally had
turned in Kent for cheating (untrue), the mad

brother from New Orleans, who now, armed,
intent on blood, is walking with harm

———

in his heart, foul revenge smoking his eye.
Vernon's own eyes grow wide. He wants to try

to hide his brother pledge at Sleep And Eat.
He knows what Kent can do enraged. He leaps

up at the sound of smashing at the door.
"Open up!" bellows Kent. Good Vernon throws

himself before Wally, who tries to flee
out of the window. No luck. "You turned me

in, you traitor." He points the pistol smack
at Wally, and then pulls the trigger. CRACK!

The victim grabs his gut and blood spurts red
between his fingers. Down he falls like lead

on the freshman dormitory floor, all dead
our bro knows inside his heart, dead, dead, dead.

*　　　*　　　*

Well, Wally recovered, washed the stage red
off, sent his clothes to the laundry. His bed

still looked much like the Saint Valentine's Day
Massacre. Kent laughed and laughed, Vernon, pale

and faint, had to sit down, but he laughed him-
self to scorn at how hard he had fallen.
Then probably we all went for a can.

Legal drinking back then began at sen-
sible sixteen, scarcely a cardinal sin!

Alas, the word did reach Our Grand Dean, who
was not amused. He did not laugh. He flew

not into a rage. But he was not amused.
The Dean himself did not drink. He had a rule:
"A gentleman may never look a fool

in public." A simple rule: "Don't be drunk
in public." The four of us were slam-dunk

safe, thought we. It was just a can after
a prank among frat-friends, good ole laughter

the college way. Alas, the word did reach
the Grand Ole Dean, who said, "I guess we'll teach

GUNS IN THE DORMITORY isn't a joke."
The lads were rusticated, that is, lo-

cated elsewhere than the freshman dorm, locked
out for a week. But we still thought we rocked!

*   *   *

Strange, though, I never got my dad to see
how great a joke it was. He never joined me
with a smile – but he must have laughed inside,
right? Right? He must have, had to've, laughed inside!
Right?

*   *   *

ODE TO BEULAH (W&L 1956-1957)

There's Beulah, blind Beulah, our landlady
junior year. Her favorite was heady

Vic from Danville, some years out but not from
the University, no, another one

which welcomed boys with zip. Vic had climbed up
the walls of Washington Hall with a buck-

et of paint and painted the General "black
as his slaves" (in Vic's words). But Fred was at

the ladder when Vic got down in the ground.
Yep, Fred the Cop was holding for the bounder.
So another college had to be found

for Vic to finish his studies. Beulah
told the story many times. To fool her

I'd tiptoe in when she was resting. "Hey,
Beulah! It's me, Vic! I was passing by,
wanted to eat a PBJ with my

favorite gal!" I whispered in the ear
of the blind old lady. But she could hear

plenty good. "Why, you're not Vic! These old ears
can hear just fine. They're better than my teary

old eyes!" One day when we came in to cheer
her up as she rested in her bed, "Hear

this, my lads!" she cried. "I've just seen a bank
of roses above my bed! O Lord, thank

You, thank You! What beautiful red roses!"
Beulah's room where she lay was warm and cosy.

She was not bitter in her blindness. My
housemates (one a fugitive from a high
-ly praised college called the Wildcats) and I
usually did more than our best to try
to make her happy that she was alive.

The story was that her department store
at Main and Washington more than forty
years ago was stolen from her. It tore
her heart again. Widowed twice, she nursed sores

of solitude. But Vic came, she's alive
again. He was her son, her only child.

With us too she was glad to be alive.
There were shocks though. In the kitchen a tribe

of cockroaches ruled the night. In daylight
they vanished, but they were quite a grand sight
if you turned the switch on for a midnight

snack. And here is where the PBJ comes
in. One night, snack time, Beulah, famished, runs

into the kitchen and makes a peanut
butter and jelly—that's crunchy peanut
butter—sandwich. Not there's really noth-

ing strange about that, is there? But who rules
when the lights are out in ancient Beulah's

kitchen? Alas, the tragedy is clear
before your eyes, and ours when we boys, fear

-ing nothing, clicked the switch on Beulah's
fearsome sandwich, which she shared with the rulers

of the night, unseen by all but our young
eyes. And heard with our young ears. "Crunch, crunch"
                                                    sung

out in that *tableau vivant*. It's a pict-
ure that we will carry beyond the kiss

of death. Beulah's came soon. Her singing Christ-
mas card—a choir of penguins!—marked DECEASED
returned the Jan. after we were christened

BA or BS (both?). She waits for Vic
up above. Let's just hope her terrific
PBJ (Roaches in Heaven!) can be fixed

above to give the Lord a Laugh Magnifique!

                    *   *   *

ODE TO MRS. WAGNER

Mrs. Wagner was our housemother at Sleep
And Eat, a smart lady who could repeat

many moving passages by the Bard—
not just "To be or not to be"—by heart.

She was so Desdemona, Othello's
star-crossed lady, herself. She felt D's woes

and the young men before her hardly chose
the Oh's they sighed from head down to their toes.

Once she had acted on the stage. Just her
appearance at a door—if there were per-

sons present—was an entrance, a grand en-
trance that those who saw it just once remem-

bered for many a day. It comes back now
as I type the words. Her memory, how

she sat head of the dining room table—
we ate on tablecloths—brothers weren't able

to believe that at our fifteenth reunion
in hippy seventy-three, and not one

necktie was to be seen on those young men
either. Après moi, le déluge—spoke French

she did too. She ruled l'ancien régime.
We lads all felt fortunate in that scheme

of things. She taught us manners, grace. One more
story! Her apartment on the first floor
was under Whit's room. One time, when his door

was open, there were several brothers
using vocabulary their mothers

never taught them, and loud too. Mrs. Wagner
appeared at the door and hurled a Wagner-

ian, "I can stand a lusty Goddamn now
and then, but this is too much!" at the crowd,

who lowered their eyes and begged her pardon.
In later years, after manners were gone,
or at least muted, the institution

of fraternal Housemother gone, no more
Mrs. Wagners were to be found. The lore

of such a lady civilizing young
males is only by latter day bards sung,

hoarse oldies of the iron. Silver?
No, just hoarse, iron voices bewildered,

trying to set down in rimed couplets rude
moving pictures of those days in a trued
and honest tongue. But can we ever our lewd
palaver lose?
                    Yet something of the mood
              may return, one or maybe two
              moments from yore to move a few.

*   *   *

ODE TO DR. FLOURNOY

Dr. Fitz Flournoy, back home after his Rhodes,
buys a Model A with a sun-roof, loads

the driver's seat with books so when he drives
his head, great mane in Virginia sun, rides

high through the hole. He's his own periscope.
He tootles down the streets reciting lop-
ey lines from the Miller's Tale, lopey dop-
ey "Tee hee quoth she, and clapped the window

to," toots out to Goshen Pass for a dip—
admits that's where he grades the papers, up

to his chest in water, a float his desk,
more of a floatlet, his pencil his best

friend in striking out the weak and adding
action verbs. "It flies!" he wrote. "No padding!"

when I was doing the latter to show
a ponderous ascension in dough-

y prose. "I wrote this lecture on Shelley
standing in the waters of the Maury,

my simple escape from the heat of the summer,"
he told us when we reached that mighty sinner

and learned the swell word "rustification."
You'll go far in life with information

———

like that! We always heard that being an
English major wouldn't keep you from any-

thing that you really wanted to do bad.
Dr. Flournoy read the lines of that cad

Iago so we felt deep in our heart
that he was Satan the devil incar-

nate. His Desdemona brought tears for our
beautiful, wronged sister. Gentle power

or strong for good or bad—in graduate school
I near blamed him for inspiring this fool

to study higher. Though 'twas Chapel Hill
it could be gray. Once to escape the mill

I even asked the draft board at home about
signing up. The woman was looking out

for me, oh bless her heart! Once she had been
a patient of my father's. "It'd be a sin

for you to don the khaki! Do you know
what boredom is? Army camp can be slow
as Texas, and I know that's where you'd go!"

Then I remembered brother John's letters
from Army camp in Texas, bitter letters

that said just that. Half drunk in border towns
made it no better. Just hot drills and sounds

of KP slops, more drills, more rifle shots

and fights in the barracks, time in the brig—
all things considered, I think I can dig

one more dull class or two in Chapel Hill.
Then I remembered auditing, the thrill

Goethe, Old Irish, Catullus, just
   the pleasure of learning
   without grading!
That was the secret. Why sure! Yep. That must

be it. The kind lady in the draft board
was waiting still my thoughts on Texas Bore-
ing. "Daddy'd bless you!" I was out the door.

My draft card's still, quite still, in my wallet.
"Afghanistan" I hear. Wait! My talent,
though slight, could it've been used if I'd been sent?

Never worn a uniform isn't to brag
about. Watched Hogan's Heroes in Stalag

and dreamed, but still too young for Korea.
Too old for Vietnam. "Don't ya see ya

could have been John McCain, hero, next Pres-
ident of the USA?!" you say, press-

   ing my old friend on me a bit.
   You've got me there I must admit.

———

My roommate Salvadore in Chapel
Hill fought in Korea. In sleep, his hell,

he saw himself throw the grenade that killed
an enemy soldier. He did as drilled

and lived a killer in his mind through life.
I guess I'd rather give assignments rife

with blood and busted heads in Scott and By-
ron than try it myself. Where lies the lie

in all of this? I know it's here somewhere.
But I'm retired! No longer do I care!

MORE MEMORIES OF CHAPEL HILL

Required were French and Latin, Old English
and German. Old English was what finished

careers at Chapel Hill. Or Beowulf—
both taught by Dr. Eliason. Tough

was his middle name. There were no grades when
I first arrived in fifty-eight. Hey! Lend

me your ears! That was fifty years ago
next fall. I just subtracted! At the o-

pening reception Mrs. Holman looked
at the two of us hard: "You know that books

are not real life." She was the chairman's wife.
We lads were fresh from college. Such a knife

from such a lady we did not expect
on opening day. We could hardly deflect

that cold charge. Her husband had grown
up as a sharecropper's son in a home

unlike my own in genteel Virginia.
Washington and Lee did hold a sinner

or two, that is true, if puppy sins count.
Didn't know mortal vs. venial—doughty

lads that we thought ourselves to be. But
unspoiled we were not. Okay, sheltered, lucky
we were, not grown up fast by Vietnam, but

we weren't strangers to death in a fast car,
alas. Yet when we got as far as Tar-

heel land, schooled by Dr. Flournoy we knew
that Bard was life, real life in giant boots.

Mrs. Holman's first bite caught us off guard.
Yet Doc Eliason brought that which marred

Arcadia. 'Twas the beast Old English
or Beowulf that thinned the flock, finished

off hapless graduate students. There were no
grades, just Pass and Fail. A pass or a Low

Pass was just fine. But a C was an F.
If you dropped below that thin, thin line, if

you slipped just once, we'd throw a grand party
and help you pack like Bubsy's farewell hearty

when he tootled off to Tulane. No harm
was done because everyone in this charmed

era would have a job as teacher soon.
"Demand exceeds supply"—it was a boon

time for teachers. That would change forever
in nineteen hundred and seventy-four.

"Supply exceeds demand"—the system craved
instructors who could teach freshmen. That saved

the mighty profs from composition one.
The system did not check itself. Undone

in time, it sent PhDs to Denver
as taxi drivers, it was said more there

than any other city in the land.
Well, the climate's just ideal for a fan

of skiing, right? But have you gotten a
sad letter from an old student, an A

student, now a gypsy with a PhD?
Administrators, deans, and the like see

sly possibility here. Save a buck
or two. The number now on tenure track

is down percentage-wise. Guess who loses.
You got it. Students in the classroom whose

instructors aren't still there when a letter
of recommendation is sought. Better

than a GPA are words by a friend
who taught you maybe more than once that lend

a soul to the profile of the aspirant.
But how'd we stray into words so indifferent

and Latinate? We must get back to Story!
May Dr. Eliason provide a gory

fable from the tables of Lenoir Hall,
the home of the forty-cent student all-

you-can-eat special, coffee free after
the first nickel, a scene of jokes, laughter,

and grad students talking with their teachers.
Well, Jim was a student with rare features

in class with us. He was a charming guy,
popular and smart. He had lost an eye
in youth and sported a glass globe of high

gloss, which he liked to show off. At coffee
one day he chanced to sit with Dr. E.

The subject of glasses eyes in Anglo-Sax-
on times arose. (Believe!) The Doctor asks

if he might see a modern eye up close.
"Of course," says Jim in a manner almost

brave, for he was not alone in fearing
the stately Doc. Out comes the eye glaring

from Jim's cupped, shaking hand. He holds it out . . .
but stretching to hand it over, without

warning it hops right in the coffee cup
of Doctor E., who looked first down then up.

That's where the memory stops. The rest is seen
alone. Who called for help or washed it clean?

How memory stops short Wordsworth taught us
in spots of time. The man's body brought us

bolt upright into the boy's look: the drowned
man's face, the girl's garment vexed by the wind,

the brothers trailing their father's coffin.
Such black and white close-cropped snapshots seldom

last as long as your mind. So you had better
put them on paper or a disk for later

generations in the family when
the mind or breath begins to grow too thin

to claim you are alive. Back to fable!
So grave we were I'm almost unable

to cook up escapades in Chapel Hill
outside the library. True, there was a thrill

or two up in the stacks amongst the books
and old bound journals, something beyond looks

scholastic, proposals with or without
engagement rings. "Pizza, Miss?" "How about

a cup of java, dear?" That's racy stuff
when you've been reading John Donne. Not much fluff

in carnal or in pulpit Donne. J. O.
Victorian Bailey was another hero,

———

a man who did the work of any four
common mortals. His office on the first floor

was open that wild day when students bawl-
ing ran riot and dashed through Bingham Hall

smashing windows and doors. Dr. Bailey
was sitting at his desk at his daily

work in the vineyard of the Lord. He didn't
give a glance. A student yelled, "We ain't kiddin!"

and broke the window of his door. Vietnam
protests hit Davidson too, but calmer.

Ah, the remembrance of things past. It's time
to shut the door on Chapel Hill. A crime!
You say. Or maybe not—so darn much rime!
All right. Honestly, I'm not paid a dime

for all of this. So let's close on a note
of sadness. It is not manly to dote

on the passing of a friend. Restaurants
do close their doors for good—like folks, they can't

live forever—but the Ratskeller! The Rat!
Please, please, say it ain't so! We chewed the fat
at that table by the belt where we sat,

the conveyor belt that carried baskets
of garlic buttered toast there for the asking!

And so must die this slight song on the Rat
and snaps of The Hill that are mostly fact.

If you don't hear the sound of verity
(it's late to ask the actors
or witnesses about the factors)
just give a foot or rime or three of charity.

EVERGLADING

more heroic couplets murdered by J. G. H., from July 8, 08, on

One hundred years ago the family tripped
out of Chicago all the way to vir-

gin Florida, Miami, popula-
tion under fifty thousand we did say

for generations, and nary a hut
on Miami Beach. The latter's true, but

a little digging after Cora's birth—
she's named after my Grandma, Daddy's moth-

er, the one grandparent I knew, we found
the count was not fifty, more like around

five thousand plus a trillion trillion mo-
squitoes. My grandfather had a plan for

developing the Everglades. (Grandma:
"Grandfather doesn't exaggerate at all.

He just sees things bigger than anybod-
y else.") So out into the swamp we'd boat—

I trust with guides—and dream. The trouble was
that after every trip—for the dog's nose

was too inquisitive—we'd have to get
another dog! No, no, not alliga-

tors (I know what you are thinking!)—water moc-
casins! Fidodo would stick his nose out

too far and moc would snag it.
You'd have to call that tragic!

One Fido after another got mocked.
My Uncle Charles's letter had been locked

away with family papers until just
a couple of years ago. Granddad must

have kept after the plan to develop
the swamps for years. The Canadians dropped

supporting the swampy scheme when they thought
World War One was not being wisely fought.

Canadian money'd been behind it all.
I've treasured Uncle Charles's letters, scrawled

in his wonderful script and filled with wit.
But this one was typed and perhaps a bit

more—not formal
but say historical.

One prize picture postcard is from Aunt Anne
and Uncle Charles honeymooning Hava-

na style. In California they often
headed south of the Border for some fun.

"Marry me and I'll show you the world!" is
one bit of family lore we hope is

so! One memory stands bright as a cedar.
When I was little when we decora-

ted the Christmas tree, the star on top al-
ways was saved for Uncle Charles to install.

He came with Florida fruit. The modest
cumquat was smuggled in (sly!) with the best

of oranges. The royal coconut
was sacrificed for its milk, which brought luck.

Ah! mangoes! This is fruit to capture your
fancy! The avocado eaten pure

with lemon for an appetizer we
today still share. Desserts? Pecan pie, le-

mon pie. Around the table were mellow
moments—but back to the Canal! Yellow

fever the mosquitoes used to fight us
till the Pacific cleared a cruise of trust

for the whole family of four to set sail—
was it '14?—up the coast, then by rail

through Canada east to Glacier and loch
and stayed at Banff Springs Hotel à la Scotch

Baronial Castle, built in eighty-eight.
Our family crossed its Persian rugs in late

spring of seventy-one, mused o'er the time
of Daddy's visit as a boy, to find
last year when searching the past for a line

for Cora Gill, as said named for Grandma,
our hotel burned in twenty-seven—we saw

the spectral double built in twenty-eight,
but just to walk its high rooms, wasn't it fate

enough for us? Back then there were giants
in the earth! We five could not quite finance

a night in Banff Springs Hotel but settled
for a B&B whose host the kettle

kept whistling every hour of the day.
We noticed that Norwegian journals lay
about. Years before she'd come from Norway's

far north. Widowed, "Neither place is complete
now. Parts are missing. So I stay and meet

my guests. One hears that Norway's people read
the most. Those dark long winters are the key—
no puzzle why. Bring me Hamsun and Lie,
a lamp, a corner fireplace, I'm as free

a soul as any in the world." Admire
her we had to. The children caught her fire

too. Wouldn't my father have been her age?
It's strange to wonder how wonder-filled days

———

might've been if he had lived to meet my bride
and hold his grandchildren. Maybe he cried

above. Remember I do when Grandma
died. Daddy in his reading chair—I saw

but more I heard him weep. "I did not do
enough for her." What did he mean? All through

my boyhood she would stay long stretches with
us in Lynchburg, Virginia. She seemed blithe

to me, playmates, full of jokes and unique
tricks all her own. You'd surely have to seek

far for a grandmother who could repeat
for the neighborhood boys just for a treat
the whole alphabet backwards lickety-

split. Maybe it was I who had somehow
failed her? That's silly. Love's stronger top down
from parent to child. That's why Chinese kow-

tow to their elders. It makes for reci-
procity, another sturdy princi-

ple from the Middle Kingdom. (By the way,
you've surely sensed this game of peregrina-

tion—the Chinese word translated here as
"Middle" comes from "bull's eye"—the arrow has

at the beginning of writing just hit
dead the bull's eye of the archer's target.)

It all comes home—the only son and son's
son in the family. Stories open, "Once

upon a time"—which reminds me, I've got
to write a story called "The Face"—a lot

of words: one fifty!—"of the Horse"—a ghost
story for The Spectator's column hosted

by Lucy Vickery. Later: that tale
has flown off to London. May it not fail

to send 1-4-9 chills (one for each word)
throughout her frame! May it not be untoward

in its reception!

THE FACE OF THE HORSE

The children laughed at the story of Jim, the horse with the
moving lips at Camp Virginia. I dreaded riding lessons. The evil horse
counselor always put me on Jim, who knew I was scared of him. In the
final show, with a whinny and a shake of his head, Jim tossed me. I lay
on the ground. The evil counselor ran over. I didn't move.

I didn't tell the children that a boy died at the horse show. He
broke his neck.

Now little Vic was going to Camp Virginia. "Pappy, do you
think Jim with the funny lips is still there?" "Oh no, my boy. He's been
glue for ages." Vic giggled, but the face of Jim haunted me. I could
hear his whinny. He might have stepped on my head.

The boy left. Dread filled me. The telephone call came the
second week he was gone.

Later: It fetched Hon-
orable Mention? Hm. That summer of long
ago! We pitched our tent June first along

a lake that was still frozen up in Gla-
cier National Park, Alberta. Snow was scraped
away to pitch our big tent. That snow made

a dint on others too. A park ranger
had put his car up under a danger-

ous looking bank twenty feet tall, took a snap-
shot to show doubters from the East who hap-

pened to shake their head at such a marvel—
or maybe he just wanted to startle

the kids with a tall tale. We crossed by boat
just at Nanaimo on Vancouver, floated

over on a ferry, saw the San Juan
Islands, the boulevards of the town won

by Astri, that is, it was named for her
we must have joked. In Seattle we hur-

ried to a motel after the soaked tent
was stuffed into Torino. The rain sent

us flying. Bergen isn't Seattle's
sister city for nothing. The tattlers
say that every baby that babbles
in Bergen's born with a brolly. Rattle

178

on down the highway south to Oregon
for a visit with brave Aunt Nell, who'd gone

into a home in Mount Angel. We dreamed
we'd gone to Germany. Every field streamed

with rows and rows of hops. Timbered houses
spoke of Bavaria. We asked locals, "How's

the beer," and got a ready grin. Inside
the home we learned Aunt Nell was biding—

       FLASH—INTERRUPTION—just met Glynn Lewis
       from B.C., a Vancouver lad who is
       Barack Obama's man on campuses

       across the States. Today's his first visit
       to Davidson. We had BBQ and fidgets

       with Bill and Earl over Hillary Clinton,
       for we're all (except me and John) bent on

       Obama for the land. The Soda Shop
       could not've been better. It is simply tops

       for meeting folks. I told the college grad
       Vancouver back in seventy-one had

       been in my thoughts yesterday (see above).
—her time (back to Aunt Nell)—"She's in the club

room down the hall." The door swung open on
a poker game of older gentlemen

              ——

around the table. Nell wasn't in the game
herself. She held the cards for one so lame

and palsied he couldn't hold his own. So she
held his for him. Back in her room we'd see

reminders of their life in Montana.
A Curtis photo of a teepee a-

dorned one wall. I asked where Cousin John's hung.
"I could not bear to have it up," she sung

out sad. "He died at fifty." That strong man
who in fifty-nine showed Hungry Horse Dam

to Mother, Aunt Mary, and me? He'd been
on the job working as the superin-
tendent when it was built. "Nobody's in
the concrete here," he told us. "A foreman
once slipped off, but he caught the very end

of a long rope that he'd tied to a cleat
on top. He dangled o'er hundreds of feet

of air." Did he walk up the concrete face
or—out too far—slowly—he did not race—

hand over hand haul himself up, over
the lip, and take the rest of the after-

noon off? In fifty-nine I got a hair-
cut in Kalispell. I was in the chair

when a cowboy came in. He was a bear
of a man. He sat. Not a word I swear

for five minutes. The barber finally said,
"Howdy." The grave man nodded his great head,
took his time, but eventually he did

reply the same. "Howdy." And that was it.
One slug does it—when you shoot straight, you hit.

Another ghost from our visit to Mount
Angel I cannot lay. "Our John, our crown,

was very ill as a boy [was it diph-
theria?]. All we thought about was death.
John's younger brother—his nickname was Biff—

we lived on a lake back then—rode his bike
off of the pier and drowned. We couldn't even cry
for thinking of John," she said with a sigh.

In fifty-nine Aunt Mary and Mother,
both recently widowed, and I weathered
the long drive to Montana, moi chauffeur,

with jokes and tall tales from Scottsboro, AL,
where they had grown up sisters. Mary, all

alone then, both her parents taken off
(perhaps influenza?), orphaned, she sought

a home with cousins step- and half-, my grand-
father'd married a widowed mother. Grand-

mother'd died when Mother was six, so there
were tales aplenty for the ride to where-

soever was Montana. Daddy's Aunt Nell
and Uncle Torrence said, "Yes, Kalispell!"

to promise of a practice if he'd coach
their semi-pro baseball team. The white folks

had settled "when the Indian Territor-
y opened up." ("What might that mean?" does your

conscience ask?) Uncle Torrence'd played baseball
before he'd gone to law school. So they hauled

the family from Chicago to Blackfoot
lands up near Canada. Yep. Sure enough
he coached the team and spent some winter months

at baseball camps in Arizona. He
became at last a Federal Judge. So the

good folks that offered him the chance to try
the West were true to promises made. By

the time we landed half a century nearer
the pioneers into the golden years'd

retired. "A hearty welcome to you! Hop
in the Packard all five of us! We're off

to Glacier!" And off we were! Up, up, up
with a deep drop on the right side and bluff

on the left, Uncle Torrence at the wheel.
That long, black Packard stretched—it had a feel

for Going-to-the-Sun Road. I must have rid-
den shotgun in front with the ladies hid-

den way in the back seat. At eighty Unc-
le Torrence drove like NASCAR. Mother sug-

gested, "Torrence, why don't you let Gill drive?"
Aunt Mary and Mother had tried to hide

their eyes behind their hands soon in the climb.
They surely did not want to hurt the fine

old feelings of the Judge. So Mother made
her delicate suggestion. The Judge said—
I can see him leaning back his grey head

with a loud guffaw—he did sense their fright—
"No-o-o, Betty, let the lad see the sights!"
So he propelled the long elastic might-
y Packard through the miles of snowcapped heights

round many a precipiced curve that lift-
ed the long Packard on up the white cliffs
that summer of nineteen hundred and fif-
ty-nine. Then Cousin John showed us the dif-

ferent views of Hungry Horse Dam and Lake.
The cherries on its banks to this day taste

———

red, but really something I can't forget
is John's friends on the lake. My mind won't let

them go. The wife had been a concert pi-
anist. Now she had just one arm to see.
Whatever had stolen the other? The c-

word. On the lake they lived with their orchard
and grand piano. Such was their fortune.

We said goodbye, and some days later told
all of these Montana tales—how we rolled

through Glacier Park—"Torrence, why don't you let
Gill drive?" "No-o-o, Betty let the lad..."—you can bet

more than once to Aunt Anne and Uncle Charles
along with so many other marvels

of Southern Cal. Then, heading east, homeward,
we stopped in Vegas. (This one should be heard.

"What happens in Vegas, stays. . . ? Read and judge!)
We heard a son of Bing sing. He had much of

his father's voice. 'Twas pleasing to the ear.
But memory hangs on her who brought my beer

and Coke for Mary and Mother's bourbon.
The lady wore no top. There she stands on
my left, the stage behind. I am so stunned

I willfully tip her one half-dollar
of silver. She shakes when she collars

the coin. I can't recall what Mother said,
but do recall once she got up and fled

at a certain scene in And God
Created Woman. (Why in the world did we see that

together?) Why don't they still make those half-
dollars today?—I think it's time to get

                            back on track fast!

We said good-bye to Aunt Nell. Her dear smile
is on our family wall. She has a child
beside her here, here and here. Dear Aunt Nell,

you're still with us all the family here
where we pass morn and eve year after year.

So on we drove. The girls had their barbies
way back in the Torino. Gill read. Hardly

even noticed them for miles. Unless there came
a sight. In seventy-five we saw flames

near Las Cruces. A car was burning road-
side. People were just watching it. We rode

on by. Police were there. New Mexico
had more to awe. A half mile off the road

———

alone all by itself there stretched a span
of bridge which was attached just to bare land—

in this one case, bare desert. Measured wrong
I guess. "But the blueprints put it along

that line!" said the red-faced sweating boss man.
How'd the railroad rails ever meet in Kan-
as drive the Golden Spike? [The reference

desk says that is not history. But rime
is what we're after! In verse you know crime

is of a different sort, for Pete's sake!
Let's write Aunt Anne and let these fool rimes shake
themselves out all by themselves! Time to take

a break!]

In seventy-five we had a two-door
hatchback Opel with special guests from Nor-
way, two grand ladies, tante Ruth and Mor-
mor. Mrs. Grundy was an orange color

with space for luggage up on top.
The plan: AM load our roof, tie with lots

of rope the bags for seven voyagers.
PM untie lots of rope undeterred
by grips or gripes—au contraire!—with laughter
unload the roof, empty the circus car—
the seven of us were a bit younger

back then, the check in (no, no, no tent for

186

us on that trip!), take a dip, drink a drop,
then time for middag! Then hop, hop or plop,

plop into bed for stories. In New Or-
leans (to this day we still blush—for-

get we cannot) we stayed in the Cornstalk
House in the Quarter after dinner thought
we'll talk a walk to see the sights we ought

to see as young folks—yes, we did, my bride
and I we left our guests the children! Hide
your faces—they were over fifty—too
elderly t'want to see the lights! The two

Norweigan guests remained with the three kids
inside while we ran off into the ci-
ty of jazz, all over the world the ci-
ty of jazz. We will tell you right now, sit-

ting here at seven-oh a genera-
tion later, we squirm repeating, "That rates
as one of the worst things we were ever fated
to do! How can we two up for that ever make?

That summer the seven of us visit-
ed Aunt Anne and Uncle Charles in a cit-

y in Southern Cal. My bride will help me
discover snapshots from that visit. The
only one I have is Astri, Siri
Lise in bathing suits with great aunty

———

and uncle—the girls are squatting because
photographer Pop
            a better shot
                        thought he saw.

On the road there was one cardinal rule:
"No one may ask, 'How much longer (cool tool,

no?) 'fore we get there?" Another tactic
the mother of the children, sage dame's trick,

had unknown treats each day for each of us
to take the wrapping off for the surprise.

A little toy, that's all, but what a plan!
But wait! Was Pop so treated too? It can
be put like this. Just say, a brace of cans

was his surprise at day's cool close. Pop! Pop!
They still used church keys in those days of top

apopping pleasures. Sissy tabs have stolen
the show today. Now crunching cans's no bold

display of muscle like when cans were steel.
We stopped in Lake Oswego at some real

old friends, the Muirs. Just image being named
John Muir in the Northwest. A luckier name

could not be found for a salesman, could it?
Sierra Club and Teddy's mentor—wouldn't

that help a lad with goods to peddle. Sure!
He wrote great books too. Stickeen sure could lure

a reader of any age who loves dogs
with fire, plus glaciers and ice-climbing clogs.

Heyday Books you should know if you love West-
ern tales. Some books by the bed in the guest

room? Look no further. Heyday is your line.
Their website waits. We had a very fine

time with the Muirs, from model airplanes run
by radio above the yard to gun-

ning full throttle down Willamette River
with Skipper John in charge, Carolyn's liver-

mush sandwiches in the basket ("You're sure
about that?" Well, whatever Mrs. Muir

prepared did taste good riding o'er the foam
in Oregon.) Hey! We've got to get home

to sunny Califor-ni-A, hey! Hey!
But this was not our first family play-

time out West. The summer of sixty-six
some desert miles south of Salt Lake City
when we drove through Las Vegas one-oh-six

thermometers read in the shade. The week
before, disaster slowed us. We didn't seek

———

it either. Smoke surprised us as it poured
out over the dashboard. Stop, out the door,

up goes the hood, smokes smoke, "Get the canteen!"
"Dash water on an electric fire?" Pee
on it! We sat and waited, cows company.
Eventually a car came. "You will need

a truck. Will send one." Eventually one
did come. The man just peered down. Yes, the sun
smoked us—year-and-a-half lad, his mother
five months gravid, and her sister younger

—all four and half running down to Red-
lands for summer school. Today it was Wed-

nesday. School was to start on Monday in
the morning. "The wiring system's ruined,"
he mused. I ventured a question. "Sir, when—

I mean, how long will it take to fix it?"
He mused on. "I darsn't say," was his unquick

reply. A truck towed us to—where's a Utah
map? A good man worked under our car all

evening. The next morning he and son towed
us to a dealer in the next town. Own

a map of Utah in this library?
No! Son with hair slicked down—I see it real

clear. I can hear the exchange. "Thank you, sir.
How much do we owe you?" Now the doozer.

"Would five bucks be too much?" "I don't have much
money, but please let me give you ten." Touch

his hands, touch his side. We, we could have cried
over this saint. By the way, he also tried
to make a living by running the dry

cleaning establishment. Going to church
perhaps required clean creases. I've a hunch

a cowboy doesn't dry-clean his Stetson.
The dealer said, "There's only one west of

the Mississippi, one wiring system
west of the river. I've checked the list and

there's just the one. They are flying it out today.
On Saturday you're ready, but I'd say

you start real early Sunday morning." Right
on! That is what we like to do. Still night—

say four A.M.—we carry babies out asleep
and with miles behind us see the sun creep

up in the rear view mirror. Later trips
we'd stop at two o'clock for a cool dip

somewhere with a pool. Once we stopped to float
the Great Salt Lake. It worked! We soaked and soaked

but could not sink—or drink that briny brew.
Before we leave the town there's one more true

snapshot not to be missed. A Piute Re-
servation was next door. Chief and squaw ev-

ery night walked down the street to the saloon.
How did I know? A glass sold to the tune

of just one nickel. Chief with headdress walked
in front, his squaw behind. Confess! I thought
they went to drink every night. I saw
them only once, but in my mind they walk

to that saloon still, night after night af-
ter night, beer nickel after nickel af-

ter nickel, the Shoshonean people
of western Utah. Rime here? Why, Temple!

As in Morman—wait! That's Tabernacle.
Not Morman, say LDS—hey! Let's rattle

on to Redlands and teach a class before
the summer's over! So, the old Manor

House was my office. The regular prof
was off in New Zealand. Now back, he of-

fered strong advice. "Anyone who does not
move to New Zealand's a fool, but you've got

to go before you're thirty." Yes we want
to see the land down under. Its fjord, moun-

tains are indeed quite norsk, though we're in doubt

the land of Norway, grand as 'tis, can boast
New Zealand's mountain rimu on its coast,
or Maoris either, though there's the proud Samisk—

to save a trip to the word book rimu's
red pine to many—but now we must use
the time we have in Redlands t'introduce

a student named Bob, ex-merchant marine,
who taught in Sacramento elemen-

tary children. He'd sailed the China line
before the Reds arrived in forty-nine.

I asked him if the change'd been good. He more
than answered. "We were off the Shanghai shore

in the Hwang-p'u stream, standing by the rail.
I saw a bouquet floating by. It sailed

right under, all flowers, gorgeous, bright red—
'Ahoy!' I called out. 'Look, look! It's a bed!'
A little girl was floating by. Her red

dress floated in the stream. Her eyes were shut.
Her cheeks were painted bright. We leaned out, but
she floated on and on. We strained, our guts

against the rail. But she was gone. The lift
of the red dress was gone. The family gift

to the River Gods had been made. The girl'd
been sacrificed. 'Twas as old as the world

in China, the old China. Guess that's my
plain answer to your question." No, that's my

own guess. He stopped when the dress was gone. Spell
it out he would not. Can a story tell

itself? "Just trust your heart," he silently
said. For years I've tried unsuccessfully

to get my mind around that lass. Or lad.
The River God just wanted children, mad

to have a sacrifice at certain times
accorded by ritual. Tried to find

a reason not superstition. Was food
it? Did a starving family for the good

of all decide one child was blessed? "The Gods
have chosen you to join them. It's not
so hard. You will be near us all. A pot

of food is yours. You won't be hungry, dear.
Your grandma will be with you very near,

aunts, favorite cousins. Chinese checkers
will be your children's game, wei-ch'i later

with the immortals." Bob, you didn't explain
                                    enough!

One more thing about the man Bob. Profane
                                    or rough

he wasn't for a sailor. And his sounding
of Miss'ssi'pi masterpiece The Sound and

the Fury he entitled "Benjy: he
(deus) a loony." That is not quite the

right wording. "He jus a loony" became
"deus a loony," God a mad divine.

This isn't critical backchat. It fits.
When William Faulkner in Lee Chapel lit

our minds in Lexington in fifty-eight
a Hollins prof asked, "How do you create

your characters?" Faulkner, who had mumbled
his reading thirty minutes (we tumbled

in the squeaking pews, embarrassed for him),
took charge, upstepped to the mike and tore in-

to answers. "Why, I start them walking down
the road and run behind them writing down

what they do!" Hollins prof down-sits red-faced.
The dapper man from Miss. was playing, test-

ing us that half-hour. His comic contempt
was famous. When book-club ladies attempted

to ask the hick (unrecognized) direc-
tions to the writer's own farm, he direct-

ly peed against a post beside the road.
At West Point he made something of a dolt

out of the unsuspecting interview-
er. It's in Life Magazine. Go look. You

must read it for yourself. Just check the pipe.
When Benjy climbed barbed wire the time was ripe

for symbol. Faulkner, running behind, wrote
stigmata unforeseen into his note-

book. Bob took hold himself. He felt the barbs
and sensed divinity deep in this hard,

unkindly world. I kept this essay years,
but now who knows where it is? My wife's fears

are that I'll die before she does. "What will
we do with all those papers?" with a shrill

she asks, half-comic, half-not-so. Yet here
I am now, making more! Word Processor,
Hail, Mighty One! But it's time to say cheer-

io to Redlands. Two last bits, no three.
Dean Umbach, etymologist, coffee
in hand, went upstairs to work every

night on six etymologies. Happy
with two only: "Canoodle," that's sappy

for hug and kiss, from words for knot in Low
and High German; second, "Blimp," the "echo-

ic of sound caused by thumping the airship
bag with a finger," coined first by a Brit

in Navy Air in nineteen-fifteen—must
have been his finger, huh? If you'd check, just
try *Webster's New World Dictionary* first.

Two more to tell. The Shakespeare man could "throat-
sing" as Mongolians do while they feed oats

to horses on the range. I did not know
that term back then. A music prof for show

later played it blind then asked if it
were animal or mineral or veget-

able. The class was split three ways. The third
is why we left the West. Our hosts offered

us a job! We're in shorts on the lawn at
the time, picnicking while chewing the fat,

the snow-topped San Bernardino Mountains
beyond ("You'd love Lake Arrowhead less than

an hour's drive up")—Southern Cal! This must
be Heaven! "Think! You could be eating Christmas

dinner al fresco here at Redlands!" I
can see Gill's white shoes shine as he jumped high

and laughed. Alas, the gentleman knew not
that was the worst of all the things he ought

not to have said. He had forgotten snow!
Juletid uten sne og skiløp? No.
Nei! N-E-I! No Xmas for a Nor-
wegian without the night white starlit show!

One wedding anniversary brother
Bjørn gave us a sleigh ride in such weather
to make you think snow's divinest ever.

Later we learned the hippies were set-
ting fire to palm trees and fruit owners let-

ting orange groves be cut down for highways.
We made the right decision, found the way

on back to Houston, where in September
sweet Astri came into the tender world.

                    Where did you come from, baby dear?
                    I came from nowhere into here.

I learned that Friday from Douglas Houchens
(on a film & grocery run), dear friend

            (just realized the rime—some days one finds
                                    something so fine)—

Re-reading in September now. Our friend
has gone. He'd like this one. At the begin-
ning of the news last night: Jerusalem

Post Office has a clerk whose job it is
to answer all the mail addressed like this:

"TO GOD, JERUSALEM ISRAEL." 'Tis
a job that takes training. Now back to Tex-

as. Mormor and tante Lise're in town
for that September birth—timing we found

perfecto! The mayor called the thirtieth—
for all the little newborns that day a gift—

"Astri Wilhemine Victoria
Holland Day," sort of a memorial

at the beginning of a life. Hats off
to you, Mr. Mayor! Now let's catch up

with stories of my students. John Dryden
had been a US Navy submarine-

er. "Turning over in your berth first meant
you slid out and turned over slightly bent

and then back in. More memorable was
the oxygen situation because

every dogsbody smoked. You got the hint
when the cigarette in your fingers went

out. See it? We are talking in the deep!
Rick, Charles, Ed, Bill—their very souls do leap

into the mind, though we returned to Da-
vidson in nineteen sixty-seven. Dates

count and they don't count. Classes started at
the hour of seven. That early class went at

it. They had either stayed up all night work-
ing at a job or were going to work

right after class. Were they eager? Mention—
just mention, not assign, *Beowulf*. Shore

enough, day after tomorrow they'd learned
it. Charles had just left his job where'd he earned

his living at a bakery. Rick came from
Kashmir Gardens. Both his parents had come
            (That's quite a name for the ghetto, no?)
from Europe. Hungry, all these lads and lass-
es. Sometimes Bill brought something fine in glass

from the family liquor store. Photographs,
enlargements, handsome glossies—just for laughs—

of the First Walk on the Moon he mailed
to us in Carolina. We have failed

to find them but never have we thrown them
out! Ed still sends me manuscripts. Saint Ex-
upéry his hero: "Hemingway plus,

yes, Plato," he would say. He wrote he played
golf with his step-son in later years, said

he'd will me his antique shotgun. Hope I
don't outlive him. Yesterday evening high-

ball time I asked my bride what she recalled
from Houston times. "When the family would all

get in the car, haul down to Galveston.
We'd pull the car right up on the beach. Fun!"

Flash to the future—now! A witness just
agreed. "Friends say, 'You've got a beach in Hous-

ton?!' 'Yep, just forty miles away.'" "You still
park up on the beach? Great old houses still

there?" She nods. "But the ride down has all changed.
Remember there was nothing there? All changed

now, all built up." "We stayed on Padre Is-
land the summer of sixty-two. Cacti

and one motel." "It's a big resort now."
Now, September '08. Ike left this town
little, a very little, just a mound
                              of trash. Trash, and of hope only ash.
The Houston docks—there Jim Lykes showed us how

electric ships look, work in the Lykes Line.
We drove a rental truck to fetch the fine

buffet Mormor designed when she married
her Captain Tønnesen, who might have carried

her through the doorway—but is that custom
in Norway? History is still silent. It must've

been the practice on that mountain near Lil-
lihammer way back when! We listed, tilted—

thank heaven it came in parts—all by ourself
and set it up with more than pride! Had help

though when returned to Caroline. The school
picked up the bill. We hardly filled when moved

the truck, unpacked on North Main in the house
of Dean Johnston and his family in lost

years of the college. President Martin
and Dean Johnston, two great men, both led in

the grand old style of gentlemen. They knew
how hiring should be done. They also knew

how tenure worked, who was accountable
for the decisions. We're incapable

today it seems. Who is accountable
when the decision's all o'er the table

and the department's letters go to all,
and not just to the ones responsible?

But let this pass for now. Let us just say
they were indeed fine leaders, but, but may-

be they did make two mistakes. Nobody
is perfect, even the best. —They hired me
two times! We are grateful for those truly

merciful gentlemen, though they winked twice.

These days, following the set law of life
and my bride's sweet injunction, "Dump the trif-
les thousandfold down in your office, mice
don't need a cozy place to hide and slice

off bits of notebook, photographs of cra-
zy gone amigos, letters now too late

to answer." Thank heavens Brad's kept the fam-
ily tree in Alabama. At our grand-
father's funeral I met half-uncles and
far-flung kinfolk—Half-Uncle Ben made an

impression on my young soul. He had served
the Army in Alaska and preferred

that life to all else—he showed me a snap-
shot of himself with dog and rifle backed

by mountains. Uncle Ben, oh why did you
do it? His good looks did him in. It's true.

He ended up a Chrysler dealer in West
Palm Beach and married to the very best

society had to offer of glit-
ter and of glamor! Did Alaska flit-

ter through his heart at the club? Or in his
convertible with his blonde right at his

side. Maybe deep-sea fishing gave equiv-
'lent salty thrills. His sister may live,

my mother's half sister, Jessie Wilson,
I met once in Columbia—Mother's on-
ly look-alike exactly ten years young-

er—and her mother whom I must have called
Mrs. Howland, who's not buried by—but all

this is forgotten among cousins lost
in the wide world. But let's give this a toss

and land in Scottsboro for episodes
less memorable for forgettable odes

and spike the tale with laughs. My cousin Roy
and I are in a snap at four I saw

in an ancient album not long ago.
Aunt Mary and my mother—you do know

how they could laugh together—they called it
"The Gentleman and the Prizefighter"—pick

which boy was which! A hint! What's "roy" in French?
We're posing in the yard. Behind, a ditch

204

that same summer visit was being dug
by two laborers I went out to trou-
ble. At the end of the work day they both came up

to say how sad it was I was an orph-
an. How the ladies laughed and laughed often

at that wee tale. What worm turned that ti-
ny wee half-brain of mine? Little Bit! Ly-

ing in the bed at wake-up time my moth-
er waits in dread for the quick ticking up

the hall. It's Little Bit the tiny mutt
who's come to call! When tick-tock stops, kaplunk

he drops in square on Mother's bed—like Poe
the cannon ball from Owings Mills. "Up, oh

get up now, Bestepappa," shouts the on-
ly cannon ball that's known to say, "Come on

and read a book to me!" One more canine
tale is in order. Tennessee is nine

ahead of Alabama. We're in Aunt
Jean's TV room. "Our Alabama can't

lose!" Bambi'd played basketball for the Tide
and in the Coliseum beat our five
in sixty-eight when Lefty's do-or-die

three-pointers had a down night in bank-town.
Wachovia's been bought today. No more Crown

of banking. Black Monday September two-
nine two oh oh eight. And that was the true

old Coliseum. Change. May you live in
interesting times, is the ancient Chin-

ese curse, and it is a curse. I've picked out
to wear to the investment club tonight

a Slovene tie which equals Munch's *The Scream*.
What will the Wildcats say this eve? The scene
in Washington'll be front and center. Lean

times are acoming. Students dress in black
here in the library—I kid you not.
Things do not rime. I just now heard that "Facts
on the ground means SOLDIERS." A Georgian fact

of the Russian matter. It is the Thurs-
day after Black Monday. Last night we heard

the numbers at the club, the Wildcat Club,
and kept the cash. This morning bride and hub-

by walked along the rough cross-country trail
in chilly weather—and thought about Hal.

Last night we talked to his widowed Dedi
in Baltimore. He passed on so quickly

for one so full of wit and charm in May
in Lexington at our five-star heyday

five-oh reunion anniversary.
Hal told us jokes. That was his specialty.
The one about the horse in the derby

I've tried to reconstruct since that luncheon
before Doremus on the lawn. The punch

line was like, "He's not deaf. This horse is blind"—
to the astonished jockey. But on to Vietnam.

EPISCOPAL HIGH DAYS. JOHN MCCAIN '54

Since John is running hard for President
it only seems appropriate to bend

a line or two around his story on the Hill.
In Vietnam where he was almost killed

when shot down, tortured—read his own account
of "church." The prisoners were beaten, hounded

into a coughing signal. A cough stood
for "C," which stood for church for those who would

in secret serve the Lord. They worshipped thus
for months, for years. Once a guard in the dust

made "X" with his boot, quickly scratched it out.
"I'm with you all in Christ." He looked about

unsure if they were watched. It could have cost
him life. I confess that I knew almost
naught about that then. When John crashed, I boasted,

"They'll never break McCain. He was too good
a wrestler—and can he cuss!" Senior year he would

walk in my room and get my goat. I'd plead
to him, "Stop, stop. Please stop!" He did not heed

my prayer, though I cast a glance upwards
toward the ceiling. Laughing, born to such words

he was, a son and grandson of sailors.
A sailor's no sailor if he launders

his language, is he? They couldn't reach his soul
or crack their church of coughs. "Cough!" We're in hol-

iness together. Did his faith go back
to Mr. Ravenal? Now on the track

to the White House McCain credits his mentor
with his success. I clearly remember

our junior English teacher and football
coach. I can see him running that first fall

of '50 down under a kick to show
us how it's done. Mr. R. took John in tow—

John worked demerits off blow by blow
in his front yard. McCain's, when ex-PO

W, regret was he'd gotten back home
too late to see his older master. "He's gone!"

was the echo when he called. "Heart attack
at fifty-one." That was a deep regret,

he told us in his book about the war.
I drove up to Alexandria for

a rally for John back in two thousand,
wrote another check after his rousing

campaign speech. He was his old laughing self.
"Would you let Mrs. McCain help herself

to Air Force One if she were running for
your seat as Arizona Senator

if you were President?" "Why sure I would!"
He bantered with the crowd. His lines were good.
We shook hands. He pointed toward the full

bar—it was 11 A.M.—and winked.
"Gill, we would've made a mess of that (he clinked

a glass) in the old days!" But his master
Mr. Ravenel has connections here

for Davidson folk. We need to know he was
a grad seventy-three years ago, class

of three-five. His yearbook gaze tells the story
of McCain's firm friend. Live not for glory.

Just live to serve. Look at the senior's list
of deeds. In World War Two he enlisted,

209

served with honor. How sad the warriors missed
that meeting. We can hear them now,

                                   the greeting!

CASABLANCA, OR: TIME ENOUGH

PRESENTIMENTS OF SPRING IN PARIS

on the occasion of the announcement in The Wall Street Journal *of*
the filming of Return to Casablanca,
the sequel to Casablanca,
unheroic couplets by Gill Holland

It's *Casablanca*'s seventieth birth-
day and the sequel's been announced. The first

presentiments are everybody's own.
A son is born to Ilsa, Bogie's own.

We can imagine how he's turning out.
"round up the usual suspects." The krauts

are drowned out by the Marseillaise. "Play it,
Sam. Play 'As Time Goes By.'" "Louis, I think

this is the beginning of a beautiful
friendship." "we'll always have (our) Paris" full
of spring. "of all the gin joints in all

the towns in the world, she walks into mine."
Return to Casablanca is this time

around to be its name.
                              May it claim the same fame!

Heard in the Lee Hi truck stop on US 11 north of Lexington, VA:
"As long as you don't let your wants outrun your needs,
you're still in the game."

ABOUT THE AUTHOR

Gill Holland was born in Lynch, Kentucky, and grew up in Lynchburg, Virginia. He was educated at Episcopal High School, Washington and Lee University, and the University of North Carolina at Chapel Hill. He also studied Mandarin and Classical Chinese at Stanford University and in Taiwan and Beijing.

Most of his college teaching career was at Davidson College, where he taught English, writing, and Chinese and Scandinavian literature in translation. He also taught at Duke University, the University of Houston, Redlands University, Tunghai University in Taiwan, Beijing Normal University, and Capital Normal University in Beijing. He also had a teaching Fulbright at the University of Łódź, Poland. He and his wife Siri have taken students abroad to study at the University of Cambridge and Capital Normal University.

He has lectured and published at home and abroad on English, Norwegian and Chinese literature and art. In addition to poems, stories, and translations of Chinese poetry, he has published a book of translations of the journals of the Norwegian artist Edvard Munch (*The Private Journals of EDVARD MUNCH: We Are Flames Which Pour Out of the Earth*, University of Wisconsin Press, 2005.)

He and Siri have been blessed with three children and many grandchildren. The family has close ties to family and friends in Oslo.